The Essence of the Economy

PUBLISHED TITLES

The Essence of the Economy

Second edition

JOSEPH G. NELLIS
Professor of International Management Economics
Cranfield School of Management, Cranfield University

and

DAVID PARKER
Senior Lecturer in Managerial Economics
University of Birmingham Business School

Prentice Hall
London   New York   Toronto   Sydney   Tokyo   Singapore
Madrid   Mexico City   Munich

First published 1996 by
Prentice Hall Europe
Campus 400, Maylands Avenue
Hemel Hempstead
Hertfordshire, HP2 7EZ
A division of
Simon & Schuster International Group

Typeset in 10/12 pt Palatino by Photoprint, Torquay, Devon

Printed and bound in Great Britain by Hartnolls Limited,
Bodmin, Cornwall

Library of Congress Cataloging-in-Publication Data

Available from the publisher

British Library Cataloguing in Publication Data

A catalogue record for this book is available from the British
Library

ISBN 0-13-356502-5

1 2 3 4 5 00 99 98 97 96

To
Helen, Gareth, Daniel and Kathleen
Megan, Michael and Matthew

Contents

Preface to the first edition

As the world of business becomes more competitive, more dynamic and more global, there is a growing and indeed urgent need for managers to be critically aware of the events taking place in their wider economic environment. 'No business is an island' and, consequently, no manager can afford to ignore the importance of changes in the external economic conditions under which commerce and business must take place. Those conditions are not always friendly – think about the boardroom panic (to varying degrees) when headlines report increases in interest rates, inflation and taxes, or the unsteadiness of sterling. The reason for this panic is simply explained by the fact that events such as these are beyond the control of boardroom members and managers. Companies may feel they are in control of more domestic (i.e. internal) matters such as pricing policy, production levels, marketing expenditure, R&D, etc., but it is an inescapable fact that no company is able to control its external economic environment; and ultimately it is changes in the external environment that cause the death of many companies.

Recognizing the importance of the external economy on business decision making is one thing; responding to it is quite a different matter. To be able to reach sound business decisions in a dynamic economy requires managers to have a clear understanding of economic interrelationships and their impact upon business. For example, if interest rates go up, what is likely to happen to exchange rates, consumer spending, savings, prices, etc., and what will be the consequence for businesses? Or, if the balance of payments on current account collapses, what are the likely implications for the exchange rate, interest rates, taxes, etc., and ultimately, economic growth?

The aim of this book is to provide a clear and concise picture of the way in which an economy works and why different governments adopt different economic policies. This is not a book for those with a specialist interest in economics; it is a book for those interested in the economy in the widest possible sense. In particular, since every business is directly affected by economic events, every manager should find this book useful. In addition, since economics is a compulsory element in many professional management courses, participants on such courses should find the book attractive, including those on Master of Business Administration (MBA) and Diploma in Management Studies (DMS) programmes as well as practising managers attending continuing studies courses in which the economic environment of business is an integral part. The book is also suitably structured for students attending business studies and general economics courses at universities, polytechnics and colleges of further and higher education. More generally, the book is intended to provide a 'communication bridge' between managers and professional economists, and to this end we have avoided as far as possible the use of inaccessible jargon and esoteric debate.

We are indebted to our secretary, Christine Williams, for typing the various drafts of the manuscript. Again, she has amazed us by maintaining her joviality when confronted with two authors for whom the deadline for work was always yesterday. We are also grateful to our colleagues, Dr Frank Fishwick and Professor Adrian Buckley, for their advice and many helpful suggestions during the writing of the book. Thanks are also due to those students and managers who have attended Cranfield School of Management in recent years. Their contributions to classroom discussions were invaluable both in encouraging us to write this book and, perhaps more importantly, in helping us to focus on the key issues and topics.

Lastly, we are thankful to our families for their support. This book has in every sense been a joint effort, and it is dedicated to them.

JOSEPH G. NELLIS
DAVID PARKER
Cranfield School of Management

Preface to the second edition

Since the publication of the first edition of *Essence of the Economy* much has happened in the macroeconomy nationally and globally: the major industrialized nations have gone through a 'boom-to-bust' cycle of economic activity (particularly in the UK and the USA); new trading blocs have been formed (the most prominent one being NAFTA); the exchange rate mechanism of the European Community has been under intense pressure prior to and following the UK's departure from the mechanism in 1992; Germany has unified while Central and Eastern Europe have struggled with the process of liberalization and marketization. At the same time, the newly industrialized economies of the Far East have continued along an economic boom followed by a host of developing nations, including China. The balance of world economic power is rapidly changing and will continue to do so in the years ahead as the telecommunications explosion and increasing technology transfer alter the structure and relative competitive position of economies.

It is against this background that we have produced this second edition. While it has not been possible to incorporate details of all the major developments of recent years, we have taken the opportunity to totally rewrite Chapter 2 and move the focus away from the UK to the international environment, putting many of the changes outlined above into a global macroeconomic context. Much of the rest of the book remains in its original format but with all examples and statistics updated. In addition, the case studies in Chapter 10 have been revised to update the information and to include new material where appropriate.

Once again, we would like to acknowledge the administrative assistance of Chris Williams in preparing this new edition. Finally, we are grateful, as always, for the support of our families who we hope have forgiven us for our many days of absence from home.

JOSEPH G. NELLIS
Cranfield School of Management
DAVID PARKER
University of Birmingham

1

The essence of the economy: an overview

Business and the economy

The success or failure of a business is, to a large extent, dependent upon how its managers perform in terms of financial controls, marketing strategies, product design, research and development, etc. A great deal of time and effort is spent by successful firms in ensuring that the right decisions are made in a competitive environment with the greatest attention being paid to the immediate environment in which the firms are operating – to the workforce, to the production line, to the marketplace for products, to direct competitors. This immediate environment is described as the *microeconomic* environment of a firm and involves prices, revenues, costs, employment levels and so on.

There are, however, other facets of a firm's environment of which the most notable comprise the general social and economic conditions of the larger system of which each firm forms a part. Changing social values (for example, with regard to the natural environment) combined with social movements powerfully condition economic activity and, hence, the way in which companies are operated by the managers and workers within them. The political and legal frameworks of a country also have a significant impact upon the business sector and the way in which firms attempt to carry out their activities. In this book our attention will be focused mainly on the more direct economic facets of the firm's wider environment, that is the *macroeconomy*. In contrast to the microeconomy, this refers to the factors which are external to the immediate environment of the firm: it involves changes in general inflation and employment, for example, rather than changes in the firm's own product prices and workforce.

1

Macroeconomics, therefore, refers to the aggregate national and, increasingly, international economy of which the firm is a subunit.

By definition, since each firm is a subunit of the larger economic system, it is unable to exercise control over the macroeconomic environment in the way that it has control (though perhaps limited) over its microeconomic environment. Yet a plain truth stares every firm in the face: failure to adapt to a changing, dynamic macroeconomy inevitably results in business failure. Nevertheless, how many managers actively seek to keep themselves informed of the key developments within the wider economy? How many managers actively seek to monitor and forecast wider economic trends and plan investment and production accordingly? One thing is certain: successful firms pay considerably more attention to these external economic factors than those firms that struggle to survive. Ultimately, the changing macroeconomy determines growth in the nation's income and its ability to expand demand for products. Far too many managers 'keep their heads down', making sure that the day-to-day things are going smoothly. Day-to-day things are important, but success requires critical awareness and a vision of future economic prospects.

The aim in this book is to provide managers with the basic skills and understanding of the macroeconomy upon which they can build this critical awareness and vision. There are, of course, no simple right or wrong answers: instead, we hope to build a foundation of understanding and enthusiasm to learn more about the way in which the macroeconomy operates and the impact it has upon the business world in order to assist managers in their decision making.

In this chapter the scene is set for the discussion of the wider economic environment and analysis of economic principles and policy in subsequent chapters. In particular, we outline the major economic problems facing countries today and the different policy measures that governments can adopt to tackle these problems. We also consider the nature of the economic problem which lies at the heart of the study of economics and introduce the concept of opportunity cost. Lastly, we present a brief overview of the role of government in the economy. The precise degree to which governments need to involve themselves in managing the economy is a recurring debate in economics.

Introducing the macroeconomic environment of business

It is not difficult to identify which aspects of the macroeconomic environment are of greatest importance to business decision making: *all* aspects are important. This is readily confirmed by asking a group of managers to decide whether or not changes in each of the following macroeconomic variables are likely to have an impact upon their businesses (recognizing that some variables will have a more immediate and direct impact than others):

- economic growth;
- inflation;
- interest rates;
- availability of credit and monetary growth;
- total investment;
- public expenditure plans;
- taxation, personal and corporate;
- total consumer expenditure;
- total savings;
- wages and earnings at the economy level;
- employment trends;
- imports, exports and the balance of payments.

The list could be extended considerably but the message is that firms operate within an environment that is extremely complex and dynamic.

In addition, all of these economic variables are interrelated to some extent. For example, changes in monetary growth affect interest rates; changes in taxation have implications for the level of public expenditure as well as consumer spending and investment; changes in the exchange rate affect the price of imports and exports and hence can have an impact on the volume (and value) of goods traded. Furthermore, all of these variables are either directly controlled by the government or indirectly affected by government economic policies. These policies may be summarized under the general headings of:

- fiscal policy;
- monetary policy;
- exchange rate policy;
- international trade policy;
- supply-side policy;
- prices and incomes policy;
- employment policy.

The extent to which firms are vulnerable to both domestic and international macroeconomic factors is summarized in Figure 1.1.

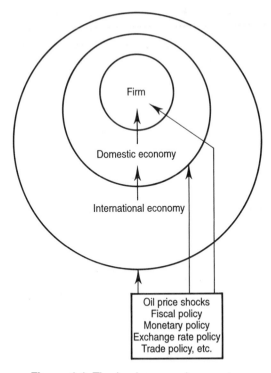

Figure 1.1 The business environment.

Fiscal policy

Fiscal policy is concerned with the composition of and changes in the levels of public expenditure and taxation. Changes in the UK are generally announced once a year. Public expenditure figures for the current fiscal year (1 April to 31 March) and targets usually for the following three years along with changes in the level and structure of taxation (personal and corporate) are announced in the Chancellor of the Exchequer's budget speech in November (prior to 1993 the main budget speech was presented in March of each year).

Monetary policy

Monetary policy is defined as government measures to influence the cost (i.e. the rate of interest) and availability of credit in the economy thereby affecting the overall supply of money. While fiscal changes are usually announced annually, monetary policy measures are continuous. For example, the government may announce interest rate changes at any time, and these rapidly affect the level and structure of competing interest rates generally (such as bank and building society mortgage and deposit rates).

Exchange rate policy

Exchange rate policy refers to government intervention on the foreign exchange markets to influence the level and direction of the external value of a country's currency. The degree of intervention depends upon the government's specific exchange rate objective: whether to have a fixed, freely floating or managed rate and, where the exchange rate is fixed or managed, at what level to 'peg' the rate. Exchange rate policy has important implications for trade and capital flows in and out of the country, i.e. for the current and capital accounts of the balance of payments. It also has an impact upon domestic monetary policy since interest rate levels may have to be set to protect the exchange rate by influencing international capital flows.

International trade policy

Trade policy involves measures taken by government, in addition to exchange rate policy, to influence the magnitude and direction of foreign trade. There may be many reasons for these measures, notably correction of balance of payments problems, preserving domestic employment, encouraging economic growth and promoting foreign co-operation (for example, within the European Union). The measures may take the form of subsidies for exports, tariffs (duties) on imports and other protectionist measures such as import quotas.

Supply-side policy

Supply-side policy arises out of what is often termed supply-side economics. It refers to those government policies that are directed at tackling problems involving the aggregate supply (i.e. production) of goods and services in the economy. Supply-side policy, therefore, contrasts with the policies described above, especially fiscal and monetary policies, which are usually concerned with affecting the level of total or aggregate demand for goods and services – i.e. the demand side of the economy. Measures used are directed specifically at influencing productivity and output costs. These may involve the introduction of new technology, the encouragement of competition and enterprise, privatization of state assets, efforts to increase labour efficiency and other measures to improve the operation of the market economy.

Prices and incomes policies

Prices and incomes policies are examples of direct intervention by government in the working of a market economy. They involve government intervention in the setting of prices for goods and services and in influencing wage settlements. These policies have two fundamental aims: control over general inflation and the protection of jobs in the domestic economy. In addition, prices and incomes policies can have a significant impact upon the distribution of income. There is a general view among economists, however, that prices and incomes policies should be regarded only as temporary or emergency measures: they distort the operation of markets by undermining wage and price levels which reflect the demand for and supply of goods, services and labour.

Employment policy

Employment policy is concerned with government efforts to create jobs and thereby reduce unemployment. The policy may be implemented either indirectly, via stimulation of aggregate demand in the economy, or directly through job creation schemes and training programmes.

Clearly, there is a large degree of overlap between these various policies and their impact upon the macroeconomic variables listed earlier. These interrelationships are stressed throughout the book. We now consider the overriding economic problem that faces governments, individuals and firms and from which the study of economics has evolved.

The economic problem

At the heart of the study of economics is the problem of how countries attempt to match the demands on their resources with the available supply. Despite a phenomenal growth in production since the Industrial Revolution, there is no evidence that, even in the richest countries, people's wants are satisfied. Although most people in the industrialized world are well fed, clothed and housed, new wants are continuously being created: the High Street is crowded with people wanting the latest fashions and electronic gadgets. Even the nature of the desirable home has changed. Thirty years ago house buyers in many Western countries looked for inside lavatories, but today they increasingly seek en-suite bathrooms and double garages. At the same time, however, for over one-half of the world's population – those in developing countries – life remains harsh. Here, basic sanitation replaces the en-suite bathroom as a priority. Indeed, in these countries there remains a desperate need for the most basic of foodstuffs and other necessities of life to ward off malnutrition and disease.

The message is clear enough: wants are limitless but the resources to satisfy them are scarce. Therefore, all societies – from the richest to the poorest – share a common economic problem involving the allocation of scarce resources to meet the needs and demands of consumers and producers. How should resources be allocated when satisfying one set of wants inevitably means another set is not met? This is equally true for individuals, firms and governments, who all face the same kind of economic problem. The individual who buys a larger house may have to forgo the annual foreign holiday. The firm that pays more to its workforce may have to reduce its investment in new plant. When the government buys more school books out of the education budget, there may be a shortage of money available to employ teachers. In other words, every decision involving the satisfaction of wants using scarce resources involves a choice. Each use of resources means forgoing some other use.

When discussing resource use, economists use the term *opportunity cost* to describe the next best option forgone. The concept of opportunity cost can be usefully illustrated in a simple diagram. The curve *PP* in Figure 1.2 represents what is called a *production possibility curve* or *frontier*. It tells us the maximum output of two goods or services that can be obtained given the current level of resources and assuming maximum efficiency in production (the idea can be extended to any number of goods or services though only two can be neatly represented on a two-dimensional diagram). The latter assumption means that resources are not wasted in producing the goods and services. To illustrate the concept of opportunity cost, assume that the two goods are defence equipment and health care services. It should be appreciated that if there are no more resources available, then to produce one unit more of something means producing less of another good (there is an opportunity cost). Therefore, if a country should decide to raise defence spending and obtain more defence equipment then the curve shows that this can be achieved only by reducing the resources used in providing health care.

The increase in defence spending is represented by a shift from point D_1 to D_2 and the fall in spending upon the health sector as a movement from point H_1 to H_2 in Figure 1.2. The reduced output of health care is the opportunity cost of achieving more defence equipment. Similar trade-offs between defence equipment and health care are shown anywhere along the *PP* curve. The shape of the curve, incidentally, reflects the fact that as

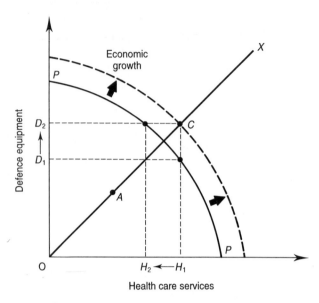

Figure 1.2 Production possibility curve.

we transfer more and more resources from one use to another – health care to defence equipment or vice versa – the resulting increase in output (of defence spending in this case) is likely to decline. This relates to the concept of *diminishing marginal returns*. It states that as we apply more of one input (e.g. labour) to another input (e.g. capital or land) then after some point the resulting increase in output becomes smaller and smaller. Therefore, for example, equal amounts of resources removed from the defence industry and employed in health care produce an increasingly smaller addition to the health care output.

It should be noted that since the *PP* curve shows the maximum production of defence equipment and health care possible with the available resources, any production combination below the curve (e.g. point A) represents an inefficient use of resources. In contrast, any point above the curve, which of course we should prefer since it implies we can have both more health care and defence equipment (e.g. point C), cannot be achieved given the current level of the country's economic resources. The obvious solution to the trade-off between defence and health care as implied by the production possibility curve is to increase the capacity of the economy to produce more of both. This is what is meant by *economic growth* and would be illustrated by an outward shift of the PP curve as shown in Figure 1.2. One objective of government, therefore, is to stimulate economic growth and hence raise economic welfare by moving the economy along a growth path such as 0X. Whether governments should attempt to do this by active intervention in the economy (e.g. through planning and investment subsidies), or whether they should simply maintain an economic and political environment in which private enterprise can flourish, continues to divide economists, much as it has done for centuries.

Government and the economy

All societies face the economic problem outlined above but they may attempt to solve it in different ways. One approach is to have a central planning body which makes all of the decisions about whose wants will be met and how. The former Soviet Union was a good example of a planned economy before its disintegration in the early 1990s. There, resource use was directed through a powerful hierarchy of state agencies headed by the USSR State Planning Committee (called Gosplan). Along with the Ministry of Finance and around nine hundred ministries and departments scattered across the Soviet Union, in principle Gosplan controlled the entire national economy of that country. The planners decided what to produce, how the goods and services should be supplied, where production should take place and to whom the goods and services should be distributed.

An alternative approach, more favoured in the West and recently adopted in much of the former Soviet bloc, is more reliance on the price or market (i.e. the capitalist) system, a system which is associated with the private ownership of resources. Instead of the allocation of resources through central planning, a capitalist economy uses prices as a signal to both producers and consumers operating in the free market. Prices indicate what and how much firms should produce to maximize their profits and they regulate how much consumers should buy to satisfy their wants. If a price is set too low, demand will exceed supply and prices will therefore tend to rise. In contrast, if a price is set too high supply will exceed demand and prices will be forced down.

In this way the price mechanism allocates resources according to consumer demand reflected in the prices that consumers are willing and able to pay. A major objection to capitalism, however, is unfairness in the distribution of resources, and it is this which led to the rise of socialism as a political and economic alternative to capitalism in the nineteenth century. In the free market economy, those with the highest incomes have more influence on the distribution of resources than those on low incomes. Each unit of money spent in the marketplace acts like a vote for goods and services. Those with the largest incomes and wealth therefore have the largest number of votes. This is not an equal 'franchise' so, therefore, central planning in which everyone (in principle) receives a more equal amount would seem fairer. In practice, however, planning has often been associated with waste and poor quality, i.e. producing well inside the production possibility curve in Figure 1.2. For example, the former Soviet Union produced two-and-a-half times more shoes than the USA but shortages of footwear continued. The shoes produced were generally of poor quality and did not last long. Wasting economic resources is equivalent to moving the production possibility curve in Figure 1.2 inwards towards the origin – fewer of all goods are produced and economic well-being declines.

In practice, all economies fall somewhere between the two extremes of central planning and completely free capitalist markets. They are known, therefore, as *mixed economies*. In the former Soviet Union, while most resources were allocated by the state, there remained a small market sector. In contrast, in the USA (generally recognized as the leading capitalist economy) there is considerable state involvement in the provision of welfare services, law and order, and defence. In all capitalist economies, governments to varying degrees aim to make the 'votes' in the marketplace more equal through taxation and welfare benefits. The extent to which this should and can be done, however, without creating economic disincentives remains controversial.

There are many reasons why governments may want to intervene in markets, even in capitalist economies. These come under a number of headings relating to:

- provision of essential services;
- transfer payments;
- natural monopolies;
- social costs and benefits;
- support for industry and commerce;
- management of aggregate demand in the economy.

Each of the reasons is discussed briefly below.

Provision of essential services

Governments may provide certain services such as health, education, policing, sanitation, etc. for everyone regardless of their ability to pay. Such services are sometimes referred to as *merit goods*: governments may regard it as meritorious or morally right to secure equality of access to such goods and services.

Transfer payments

Transfer payments are payments for which no goods or services have been offered in return and are intended usually as a means of maintaining living standards for those in society who are in most need. Examples include unemployment benefits and state pensions.

Natural monopolies

Generally, economists believe that free market competition is beneficial because it provides consumers with the maximum choice of suppliers and provides maximum incentives for firms to produce efficiently. However, governments may decide to intervene directly in certain sectors of the economy where, for technical reasons, competition cannot occur. For example, governments are likely to intervene where there are large investments in distribution systems so that it is prohibitively expensive to lay down more than one system, such as in the gas, water and electricity sectors (the public utilities). In the post-war period such natural monopolies were often state-owned: governments felt that private ownership of natural monopolies was socially and economically unacceptable. Today, however, many countries are privatizing their gas, water and electricity industries. This diminishes the role of the state but does not remove it altogether. The newly privatized public utilities normally remain state-regulated in terms of their pricing policies and service levels.

Social costs and benefits

Governments intervene to control or prohibit certain goods and services which are considered to have a detrimental effect on society, for example drugs and pornography. In addition, governments may also intervene to protect society from the side-effects of others' actions, for instance the control of pollution and the prosecution of polluters. Such side-effects (or spillover effects) are called *social costs* or *external costs*. Equally, governments often promote the supply of goods and services which are considered to have appreciable *social* or *external benefits*, for example the provision of free inoculations against infectious diseases. Government intervention with regard to control of these spillovers may take many forms including laws and regulations, fines and compensation payments, and taxes and subsidies to reduce or stimulate supply.

Support for industry and commerce

Just as governments provide support for individuals, so they may also choose to support firms. This may take the form of industrial and regional aid – notably grants, subsidies and tax concessions. Governments support firms for a variety of reasons – social and political as well as economic. The economic reasons include a desire to increase investment, to finance risky research and development, to redistribute employment, to increase total employment and to benefit exports.

Management of aggregate demand in the economy

Government may intervene to control and stimulate the level of economic activity in the economy. This is based on the view that, left to its own devices, the free market does not necessarily lead to full employment of the nation's scarce resources and therefore operation on its optimum production possibility curve. Equally, the free market might lead to high inflation. Government intervention for much of the post-war period in many Western nations was directed mainly at regulating the level of aggregate demand in the economy to influence employment and prices. More recently, attention has switched towards stimulating the supply of goods and services in the private sector (*supply-side economics*) and away from *demand management*. Whether governments should aim to control demand, especially through changes in taxation and public spending, is a major theme of this book.

Government economic objectives

Governments have a number of economic objectives, although the importance of each and the trade-offs between them vary from time to time. Several of these have been mentioned already; they are:

1. a high and sustained level of economic growth;
2. full employment of economic resources, including labour;
3. low or zero inflation;
4. a sound balance of payments coupled with a strong currency value in the foreign exchange markets.

From time to time other objectives may be emphasized such as a reduction in regional imbalances, a redistribution of income and wealth, more or less state ownership, and promotion of competition and private enterprise. The pursuance of these objectives is made all the more difficult by the existence of policy conflicts or what are often called policy *trade-offs*. Trade-offs may arise, such as between a lower rate of inflation and a higher rate of employment, in the policy measures adopted by government. Subsequent chapters explore many of these policy conflicts.

Economic targets and instruments

In attempting to understand the ways in which governments manage economies, it is important to appreciate the distinction between *policy instruments*, *policy targets* and *policy goals*. The relationship can be summarized as follows:

Targets may be defined as quantifiable aims set by governments and which governments attempt to achieve using policy instruments. Examples of policy targets might be: economic growth in real terms (allowing for inflation) of say 2 per cent per annum; reduction of unemployment by 250,000 per annum; restriction of inflation to no more than 4 per cent per annum, and so on. Once the policy targets are set, governments may choose from a range of policy instruments in their efforts to achieve them. Instruments may include changes in the level and structure of interest rates; credit restrictions and other monetary controls; exchange controls; changes in taxation, etc. A policy goal is what the government is ultimately attempting to achieve, e.g. stable prices or full employment. This distinction between policy targets, instruments and goals features in later chapters, especially in the discussion of fiscal and monetary policies in Chapters 5 and 6.

The structure of this book

In this chapter we have provided a foundation for the more detailed and structured analyses of the macroeconomy which follow. In the next chapter we set the scene for the later discussion of economic policies by providing an overview of the international economy in recent years, highlighting the record on economic growth and inflation in the major industrialized economies, as well as the future challenges to be faced as the balance of economic power changes. Chapter 3 provides a theoretical framework for understanding the interrelationships within an economy; this framework is referred to as the *circular flow of income model*. This is developed further in Chapter 4, which considers the impact of changes in certain macroeconomic variables upon the economy and the determination of the national income.

Chapters 5 to 7 focus on the major policy measures at the disposal of governments in their attempts to manage the economy: Chapter 5 deals with fiscal policy, Chapter 6 with monetary policy and Chapter 7 with supply-side measures. In each of these chapters we attempt to provide the essence of these policies in non-technical language and to identify the reasons and extent to which they have evolved or been displaced in recent years. Chapters 8 and 9 look at the international economy, and more specifically at international trading relationships, the balance of payments and exchange rate systems. These chapters are particularly relevant in the context of the current climate of increasing international economic integration, especially within a European framework, and the globalization of production and trade.

Lastly, Chapter 10 comprises a number of case studies which draw upon the material in the previous chapters. They are intended to test the reader's understanding of the economic relationships covered in the book and, where appropriate, can form the basis for group or class discussion. Readers will notice that they cover issues discussed regularly in the press and in economic commentaries on television and radio. The purpose of this chapter is to provide an insight into current economic issues which are part of the economic environment in which managers operate.

2

Developments in the international economy

In this chapter we consider developments in the international economy in the context of macroeconomic trends over the last three decades. Analysis of this nature is important in order to help managers to assess the impact of global economic trends on business and the sustainability of economic growth in the future. We shall focus on some of the major industrialized economies and provide some comparisons including developments in global trading relationships, the shift of economic power from the West to the East and the changing nature of Europe's position in the world economy.

First we shall provide a comparative review of historical trends in international economic performance in the main industrial economies up until the end of the 1980s, identifying the key drivers of economic growth. We shall then examine developments in the world economy during the first half of the 1990s before raising a number of questions relating to possible longer-term scenarios and the implications for the business environment.

International economic performance: an historical perspective

The major industrialized countries make up the membership of the Organization of Economic Co-operation and Development (OECD). Today, some 25 countries are members of the OECD, Mexico being the latest to join. Developments within the OECD over the past three decades may be broadly divided into three phases:

- 1960–73: the 'boom' years, which followed post-war reconstruction, in which there was rapid real (i.e. inflation-adjusted) growth averaging nearly 5 per cent per annum across the OECD as a whole. These years were also associated with relatively low levels of inflation and virtually full employment in most of the major industrialized nations.
- 1974–79: the 'stagflation' years, which followed the quadrupling of OPEC oil prices in 1974/5. Oil prices then doubled again towards the end of the 1970s. As a consequence, the world economy suffered a period of depressed output (stagnation) and fast rising prices (inflation), resulting in a combined effect that economists termed 'stagflation'.
- 1980–89: the years of 'structural adjustment', when growth was relatively modest in most of the developed economies. By comparison, some other economies, particularly those of the Far East, continued to industrialize rapidly, gaining an increased share of world trade. In the major industrialized economies initial deflation gave way to faster growth in the mid- to late 1980s. The initial deflation was associated with tight monetary policies that restricted economic expansion. Later, less restrictive monetary conditions led to faster growth culminating in an inflationary boom between 1987 and 1989. Throughout the decade a major feature of government policy in many countries was the restructuring of economies to achieve higher levels of productivity and competitiveness. This took the form of various government initiatives to increase the flexibility of markets, in particular the labour market, involving programmes of privatization, trade union reforms and less state intervention in the economy. These initiatives have become collectively known as 'supply-side economics' (see Chapter 7 for details).

The economic performances of some of the major industrialized economies during these three phases are examined in more detail below in terms of economic growth and inflation and also in terms of key drivers of performance such as population trends and technological developments.

Economic growth

Figure 2.1 shows the relative real GDP growth performance of Japan, the EC and the USA, as well as the average for the OECD members as a whole, during the above three periods. The key points to note are as follows:

1. All of the major economies had rapid economic growth throughout the 1960s and the early part of the 1970s, with Japan far outpacing the USA and the EC with an average annual growth rate of around 8 per cent. This compared with an OECD average rate of 4.8 per cent.

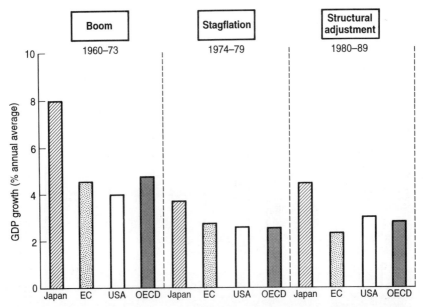

Figure 2.1 Growth rates of the major economies: 1960–80. *Source*: OECD *Historical Statistics* and *Main Economic Indicators* (note that the EC refers to twelve members of the European Community, prior to the formation of the European Union).

2. Growth fell sharply in all of the major economies after the first 'oil price shock', with the average rate for the OECD almost halving. Japan, however, still outperformed the USA and EC in this period with an average growth rate of just under 4 per cent.

3. Growth improved slightly during the 1980s in a number of OECD countries, though the rate generally remained below that of the 1960s. Japan still led the USA, while the rate for the European Community failed to match even the poor rate of the 1974–79 period. Within the average for Europe, West Germany, France and Italy had a particularly disappointing performance during the 1980s, but the UK's rate of growth improved slightly, averaging 2.3 per cent compared with around 1.3 per cent between 1974 and 1979.

Overall, it is notable that there has been a relative decline over time of the EC in terms of economic growth compared with Japan and, more recently, the USA. To some extent this is because Europe is dominated by mature industrialized economies with a large number of declining industries (such as coal mining, ship building and textiles). The restructuring of the European economies has been a major feature of policy in recent years – a

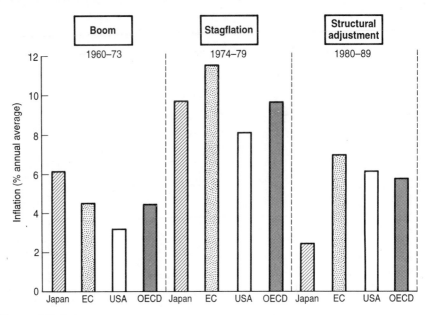

Figure 2.2 Relative consumer price inflation: 1960–89. *Source*: OECD *Historical Statistics* and *Main Economic Indicators* (note that the EC refers to twelve members of the European Community, prior to the formation of the European Union).

policy that has become all the more important given the extent to which economic power in the world is rapidly shifting from Europe to the Far East, driven by the pace of technology transfer and differential labour costs.

Inflation

Figure 2.2 shows relative rates of consumer price inflation across the same economies and over the same time periods as before. Again, the key points to note are as follows:

1. In the high growth years from 1960 to 1973, Japan recorded a relatively high inflation rate of over 6 per cent. This is not an unusual feature of a rapidly expanding economy where there is strong competition for resources as production increases. Japan's rate compares with an OECD average inflation rate of 4.4 per cent a year during the same period. The EC's inflation performance was broadly the same as that of the OECD, while the USA recorded a lower rate of around 3 per cent per annum.

2. Inflation accelerated after 1974, initially in response to the sharp increase in world oil prices. Europe was particularly badly affected with an average annual inflation rate between 1974 and 1979 of over 11 per cent compared to an OECD average of under 10 per cent and a USA rate of around 8 per cent.

3. Inflationary pressures receded sharply in the early 1980s. Throughout the 1980s Japan's rate averaged little more than 2 per cent compared with just over 7 per cent in the EC. The USA registered an average rate of about 6 per cent, close to the OECD average. Inflation accelerated again in some of the major economies towards the end of the decade as economic growth recovered. This led governments to tighten monetary policy, especially through higher interest rates (for example, in the UK, interest rates doubled from 7.5 per cent in 1988 to 15 per cent by the beginning of 1990), which in turn provoked a sharp downturn in economic activity from 1989 until the early part of the 1990s.

Overall, during the last three decades Japan has moved from having a relatively high inflation rate compared with other major economies to having one of the lowest rates. At the same time, the EC countries have generally had high inflation rates, especially since the mid-1970s, while having some of the lowest growth rates of the major economies. This change in relative performance across the major economies raises a fundamental question concerning what factors have caused this shift in the balance of global economic performance. We turn to this below.

Drivers of global economic performance

Global economic performance is driven by a range of factors that can conveniently be grouped into five categories or drivers of the world economy:

1. changes in the size and structure of populations;
2. developments in international trade and finance;
3. developments in technology;
4. changes in the availability and cost of natural resources;
5. changes in the degree of economic, social and political stability.

Table 2.1 summarizes some of the major trends between 1960 and 1989 with respect to these drivers of economic performance in the OECD. It should be appreciated that while these drivers relate to the major

Table 2.1 Drivers of economic performance in the OECD.

Drivers of performance	Boom 1960–73	Stagflation 1974–79	Structural adjustment 1980–89
Population	1.1% per annum growth in OECD population	0.8% per annum growth in OECD population	0.6% per annum growth in OECD population
	Full employment Continuing shift from agriculture to industry and commerce	Rising unemployment Decline in demand for unskilled and semi-skilled labour	Emergence of long-term 'structural' unemployment in manufacturing sectors Boom in service sector employment
International trade and finance	Development of freer international trade	Slowdown in trade growth	Global financial deregulation
	Increased national specialization	Growth of OPEC trade surpluses	Growth of regional trade groupings
	Fast expansion in world trade	Growth of OECD trade deficits	Japanese trade surpluses
		Rising non-tariff barriers	
Technology	Rapid innovation Boom in consumer durables US economic supremacy	Continued innovation and automation Emergence of Japanese technology	Rapid innovation Shorter product lifecycles Emergence of computerization and microchip technology
Natural resources	No major shocks Low energy prices	First OPEC oil price shock (1974/5) Volatility of raw material prices	Second oil price shock (1979/80) Commodity prices more subdued
Stability	Stable exchange rates to 1971	Volatile exchange rates	Attempts to manage exchange rates
	Growth and stability in the EC	Trade union militancy increases, especially in Europe	Instability in fiscal and monetary policy Growing social consequences of high unemployment

economies as a whole, particular factors will have special relevance to individual national economies, such as exchange rate movements, productivity trends and labour and capital costs. We return to some of these issues later, in the context of selected economies.

The information incorporated in Table 2.1 indicates a number of trends over the three periods from 1960 to 1989 with respect to each driver.

Population

Population growth has slowed in the OECD economies and there have been major structural changes, notably in terms of rising unemployment and a decline in the importance of manufacturing jobs. This has been associated with a fall in demand for unskilled and semi-skilled labour in the OECD countries. As worldwide competition has increased, so the balance of manufacturing employment has shifted between the existing industrialized nations and the newly industrializing countries (often referred to as NICs), especially in the Far East. The continuation of this changing balance of power, particularly from West to East, will be a dominant feature of the world economy in the years ahead.

International trade and finance

International trade has continued to expand rapidly in the face of various trade agreements which have reduced barriers to imports in most countries, although trade was adversely affected by the 1970s 'oil shocks'. These led to a short-term shift of income towards the main oil producing nations, resulting in large flows of petro-dollars as OPEC trade surpluses were invested overseas. Other features in terms of international trade and finance have been freer capital movements and the growing importance of regional trade groupings. In more recent years the emergence of trading blocs has been a dominant feature of international trading relationships, leading to developments such as the creation of the Single European Market (SEM), the North American Free Trade Association (NAFTA) and the Asia–Pacific Economic Community (APEC) in the early 1990s.

Technology

The years since 1960 have seen major developments in technology, most notably in terms of computerization of processes and, more recently, in the shape of an explosion in global telecommunications and the information superhighway. Technological change has transformed production and employment in numerous industries and has shortened product lifecycles, notably in the telecommunications and electronics industries. Whereas at the start of the period the USA and Europe dominated the world economy in terms of technological innovation, more recent years have seen Japan gain the lead in certain leading-edge technologies, notably in electronics and microchips.

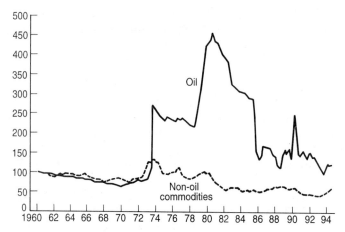

Figure 2.3 Real commodity prices, oil and non-oil: 1960–94 (index 1960 = 100).
Source: OECD *Economic Outlook*, Annex, June 1995.

Natural resources

Until 1973, natural resources placed few constraints upon production in general. Materials were readily available and relatively cheap in price. However, the OPEC price rises of the 1970s led to a period of much greater volatility in raw material costs, particularly with respect to energy. This volatility severely affected world trade, notably in the mid-1970s. The 1980s, however, saw a return to more subdued prices for both oil and other natural resources. Figure 2.3 shows movements in oil prices and non-oil commodity prices from 1960 to 1994 in real terms.

Stability

In the 1960s, unemployment remained relatively low in the major OECD economies, staying at around 2 per cent. Since the late 1960s, however, unemployment has risen as a trend, leading to more social instability. Rising demand for educated and skilled labour has widened the gap in incomes between higher paid and lower paid employees and this trend has been aggravated by tax changes that have tended to favour the better-off. Trade union militancy increased in the 1970s, though the number of working days lost through strikes has fallen in the 1980s in the face of unemployment in unionized manufacturing and a shift to the service sector where unionization is less prevalent. In some countries, notably the UK, anti-union legislation has further weakened union power. The years since the early 1970s have also been associated with considerable exchange rate instability. Up until the early 1970s, in the main, countries' exchange rates were fixed in terms of the US dollar. Since then, major currencies have 'floated' against one another (for details see Chapter 9). Foreign exchange rate fluctuations have added considerable instability to the world economy and this instability has been compounded from time to time by sharp changes in fiscal and monetary policies.

Against this background of developments within the global economy a number of national economies have been confronted with particular challenges and opportunities. We comment on some of the more significant developments:

- Japan has risen to become the second largest economic power in the world, behind the USA, with its major companies now dominating the global business environment as a result of their investment strategies and R&D programmes.
- The USA still leads the world economy with the dollar still the main internationally traded currency. Growth in the USA's trade deficit, especially with Japan, has been of growing concern and has been associated with a secular decline in the dollar–yen and dollar–deutschmark exchange rates.
- Western Europe has been faced with a number of challenges in terms of exchange rate stability, the development of a free trade area and expansion of its membership. At the same time, there has been growing pressure on the main European economies – France, (West) Germany, Italy and the UK – which have been confronted with the challenge of restructuring their economies in the face of growing international competition, especially from the Far East.

Outside the OECD membership economic performances have varied widely. Fast growth has been registered since the early 1960s in what are sometimes collectively called the 'Asian dragons' – Hong Kong, Singapore, South Korea and Taiwan (see Table 2.2). More recently, economic growth has accelerated to comparable levels in Malaysia, Thailand and China. Since 1979 China has recorded average economic growth of almost 10 per cent per annum.

In some other areas of the world, however, economic performance has been much less impressive. In Latin America growth has fluctuated dramatically, with especially high rates in the 1970s and much lower growth in the 1980s. Low economic growth, associated with rising oil prices and higher dollar interest rates, produced a 'boom-to-bust' debt crisis (for details see Chapter 10, case study 4). In the poorest of the world's economies, mainly located in Africa, economic growth has languished, leading to a growing gap in income per head between the industrial countries and these less developed nations. The problem for these poorer nations has been exacerbated by population growth frequently outstripping economic growth.

Table 2.2 Performances of the Asian dragons.

	Real GDP growth (% pa)	
	1960–79	1980–92
Asian dragons (average)	8.6	7.1
Hong Kong	8.3	6.6
Singapore	8.7	7.2
South Korea	9.1	7.3
Taiwan	8.3	7.4
Japan	8.0	4.0
OECD (average)	4.7	2.4

Source: OECD *Historical Statistics* and *Main Economic Indicators*

The stability of the world economy, particularly in terms of international trading relationships, is vital for all countries. Despite a number of crises, world economic expansion has continued over the three decades, but with periodic fluctuations around an upward trend and with variations across countries. While the general shape of the world economy has remained fairly settled over the last 30 years, there have been some important changes, especially in terms of economic integration, the increasing importance of financial flows and the rise of the economies of the Far East. As a result of these changes, there has been a growing degree of international economic interdependence. As we turn to examine developments in the 1990s, there are many more significant changes developing within the global economy, such as the break-up of the former Soviet bloc, the resulting liberalization of the Central and Eastern European economies, the opening up of communist China to international trade and investment, and the re-emergence of South Africa as an accepted member of the international community. These are examples of historic changes with profound implications, paving the way forward for many new trading opportunities.

International economic performance in the 1990s

We now turn to examine developments in the global economy during the first half of the 1990s, focusing once again on some of the major economies that make up the OECD membership. A detailed picture is presented here based on a range of key economic indicators: economic growth, inflation, unemployment, investment spending, consumer spending and international trade balances.

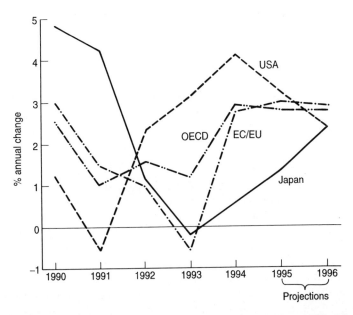

Figure 2.4 Economic growth in the major economies: 1990–96.
Source: OECD *Economic Outlook*, June 1995.

Economic growth

Figure 2.4 shows the economic growth rates for Japan, the USA, the EU countries (formerly the EC group of 12 but with three additional members since 1 January 1995) and the OECD as a whole. From the figure it is evident that all of the major economies suffered from a severe economic recession after 1989. The US economy recovered first, registering 2.4 per cent growth in 1992, but recovery did not begin in the EU as a whole until 1993/4. Japan's recession began later than elsewhere but, at the time of writing, is proving to be especially protracted, aggravated by a rising value of the yen on the international exchanges. Indeed, Japan has suffered its most severe recession since the Second World War and this has acted as a shock to national confidence.

Inflation

The severe recession of the early 1990s has led to generally lower rates of inflation across the major industrialized economies. High interest rates after 1989 reduced consumer spending and business investment. Figure

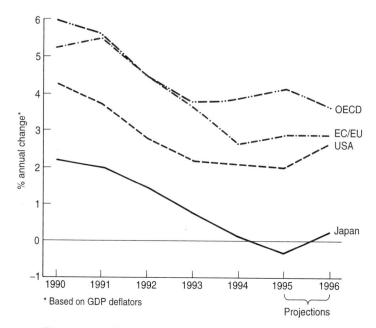

Figure 2.5 Inflation in the major economies: 1990–96.
Source: OECD *Economic Outlook*, June 1995.

2.5 shows the relative inflation rates (as measured by what is known as *the GDP deflator*). By 1995 inflation was actually negative in Japan and at a mere 2 to 3 per cent in the USA and the EU (though within the EU inflation rates have varied widely). The rate was a little higher in the OECD as a whole. By 1995, some economists were arguing that inflation was no longer a major economic problem and that governments should be paying much more attention to unemployment.

Unemployment

Figure 2.6 gives details of the unemployment rates since 1990 in the same major economies. Unemployment has grown but remains comparatively low in Japan (though some commentators argue that official figures are underestimates and that the true unemployment rate is much higher). In contrast, unemployment in the EU has been relatively high throughout the period, increasing from 8.2 per cent to over 11 per cent by 1995 (representing more than 18 million workers). The higher rate in Europe compared with the USA has been explained in terms of a 'more flexible' labour market in the USA. This leads to a greater willingness on the part of

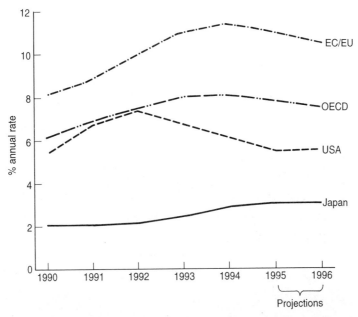

Figure 2.6 Unemployment rates in the major economies: 1990–96.
Source: OECD *Economic Outlook*, June 1995.

unemployed workers to seek jobs elsewhere. In turn, in part this is probably a product of more generous welfare benefits and the existence of employment protection legislation in the EU countries.

Investment spending

The recession of the early 1990s led to a sharp fall in investment spending in the major economies (Figure 2.7). Recovery, however, has been very strong in the USA with investment spending changing from a *reduction* of 8 per cent in 1991 to a *rise* of almost 12 per cent in 1993 and 1994. This pace of recovery is not expected to continue, however, into the second half of the 1990s. In contrast, Japan has struggled to achieve a recovery in investment expenditure, paralleling its weak economic recovery overall in the mid-1990s. By 1994, as recovery from recession was confirmed, the EU saw a corresponding increase in investment, albeit from a lower overall productive base. Given that investment in new plant and machinery represents the 'engine of economic growth', such swings in investment expenditure have important implications for future productive capacity and general economic performance.

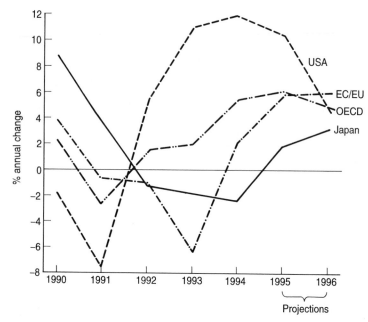

Figure 2.7 Investment expenditure in the major economies: 1990–96.
Source: OECD *Economic Outlook*, June 1995.

Consumer spending

As we explain later in the book, changes in consumer spending are an important determinant of economic growth and employment. Figure 2.8 provides data on changes in consumer spending in the same major economies during the first half of the 1990s. Spending growth slowed in the major economies after 1990, matching the overall pattern of economic activity (see Figure 2.4), recovering first in the USA. Both Japan and the EU have seen a steady improvement since the low point of 1993 which is expected to continue over the latter part of the 1990s.

International trading balances

As mentioned earlier, the world's economies have become more interdependent as a result of increased reliance on international trade. Figure 2.9 shows the balance of imports and exports of goods and services (current account balances) for the major economies, again since 1990. The figures are expressed as a percentage of the size of each economy (as measured by GDP). It will be seen that Japan continues to run large trading surpluses against the rest of the world, while the USA has large trading deficits

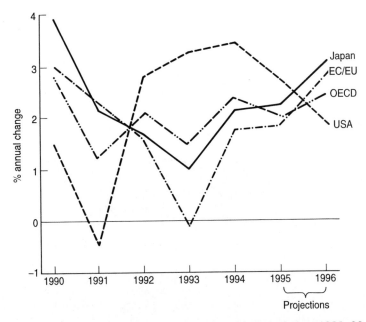

Figure 2.8 Consumer spending in the major economies: 1990–96.
Source: OECD *Economic Outlook*, June 1995.

(principally with Japan). Since 1992/3 the EU region and OECD as a whole have more or less operated with a trade balance (imports broadly equivalent to exports).

From the above analysis it will be seen that the major economies have continued to grow but at a slower rate than experienced in much of the previous 30 years. At the same time, lower inflationary pressures have generally emerged largely as a result of a much more competitive global economy, but with higher unemployment rates and continuing trade imbalances between the world's two largest economies, Japan and the USA. What these developments mean for the future of the international economy is a matter of some controversy and concern. In concluding this chapter we now turn to consider briefly some of the issues that may well determine how the future unfolds. These issues are posed as questions for debate.

Future challenges for the global economy

Our brief analysis of trends in some of the major economies of the world over the past 30 years has, to some extent, shown the degree to which a

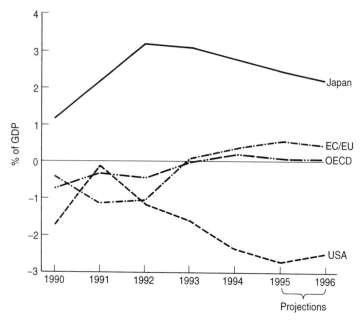

Figure 2.9 Current account balances in the major economies: 1990–96
(as a percentage of GDP).
Source: OECD *Economic Outlook*, June 1995.

shift has begun to take place in international power and influence, driven by political, economic, social, and technological factors. We now turn to future challenges for individual nations and the global economy as a whole, identifying a number of questions to be addressed under each of the headings.

Political factors

- To what extent will the business environment continue to be shaped by a changing balance of political power in the world economy, especially in the context of developments in the Far East?
- What will be the impact of increasing democratization across the globe on social and business behaviour, including consumerism and competition, particularly in the context of the developing world?
- Will political and economic reform in Central and Eastern Europe, including the former USSR (now referred to as the CIS), bring a period of sustained rapid growth in all or part of this region and, if so, what will be the implications for the Western economies?

- Is the European Union heading towards the creation of a 'political union' following the establishment of the Single European Market and the possibility of economic and monetary union incorporating a single currency and a European Central Bank in the years ahead?

Economic factors

- To what extent will there continue to be a shift in the balance of economic power, particularly from the West to the East?
- As China continues to grow economically, what will be the opportunities and threats emerging as a consequence of a new economic superpower to rival that of the USA?
- Will the post-war trend towards increasing free trade continue within the framework of the newly-formed World Trade Organization (WTO), or will the emergence of the number of strong regional trading blocs result in greater protectionism and conflict between the Americas, Europe and the Asia-Pacific region?
- What does the future hold for the economies of Africa and other developing regions as the flow of international capital concentrates on the emerging markets in South America, South-East Asia and Central Europe?
- Are the major industrialized economies facing a prolonged period of sustainable, but low economic growth in the context of a low inflation climate, or is the return of boom–bust cycles inevitable?
- Will exchange rate volatility increase or decrease and to what extent will the world continue to rely on the US dollar as its currency?

Social factors

- Will population growth in the major industrialized economies continue to slow down and what challenges are to be faced as a consequence of ageing populations, particularly in Japan and Western Europe?
- Will the economies of the Far East continue to remain as the low cost manufacturing centres of the world or will we see living standards rapidly equalize across the Northern hemisphere as economic development accelerates in the emerging markets?
- What will be the role of governments in the major industrialized nations as individual rights and responsibilities are increased in terms of social and economic welfare and environmental responsibility?

- Are we likely to see a continuation and spread of privatization policies across the globe or is there a possibility of renationalization?

Technological factors

- What will be the speed, nature and impact of technological innovation and application particularly in the context of an explosion in global telecommunications?
- Is the emergence of a 'cashless society' likely to be a reality in the near future? What effect will this have on the banking industry and society in general?
- What will be the impact on economies arising from the possible replacement of steel in cars with plastics and ceramics?
- What are the economic implications of the internet?

Concluding remarks

These questions represent only some of the many challenges facing the world today as individuals, businesses and governments strive to adjust to a dynamic global economy. Particular countries will face particular challenges. For example, will the USA remain as the world's economic leader? Has Japan reached its saturation point and is it likely to diminish in economic importance? Will China follow in the footsteps of the smaller Asian dragons and emerge as the next superpower? Will Western Europe continue the relative economic decline experienced since the 1970s with permanently high long-term unemployment? Will Russia achieve reforms in a peaceful manner or is there a danger of a major conflict breaking out?

While the purpose of this book is not to attempt to answer all of these questions, it is hoped that a better grasp of fundamental economic principles, framed within the context of the wider macroeconomy, will help managers to be better informed about the opportunities and threats which they face in the future.

3

Understanding economic flows

The essence of economic flows

As stressed in Chapter 1, managers need to understand the interrelationships within an economy if they are to appreciate the nature of the macroeconomic environment and its impact upon business. Economies are made up of a multitude of economic agents, performing varied roles within the economy in terms of both the production of goods and services and their consumption. Within the economy as a whole, economic agents may be aggregated into one of five broad groups or sectors:

1. the household sector;
2. the firm sector;
3. the government sector;
4. the financial services sector;
5. the foreign sector.

In the study of economies, these sectors and their roles are usually described as follows.

The household sector
At the most basic level, households provide the resources (factors of production) that firms need to produce goods and services. These resources take the form of labour, land and capital (both physical and financial). In return, households receive from firms payment for these factor services in the form of wages and salaries, rents and interest, profits

and dividends. At the same time, these 'incomes' generate expenditure on the goods and services produced by firms: this is referred to as consumer spending or simply as consumption.

The firm sector

In contrast to the household sector, firms employ and reward the factors of production provided by households. The employment of these resources gives rise to the many different types of goods and services produced in an economy which are then bought by households, the government, other firms and foreigners. Firms also perform a vital role in the economy in the form of investment in new plant and machinery, land and buildings and other productive capacity.

The government sector

Governments perform a number of functions within economies. Like firms they are providers of certain goods and services (for example education, health, defence and law and order) and they pay wages to their employees who form part of the household sector. They also purchase the final goods and services of firms thereby adding to total consumption expenditure, and carry out investment through the building of new roads, hospitals, schools, etc. Lastly, governments collect taxes from individuals and companies to finance their expenditure, including making payments (known as *transfer payments*) out of taxation to the unemployed, pensioners, students, the sick and so on.

The financial services sector

This sector of the economy comprises the full range of financial intermediaries – banks, building societies, insurance companies, pension funds, etc. These institutions do not produce any physical (tangible) output and therefore they are usually grouped separately from other firms. They play a vital role in the economy by providing services which channel money from savers to borrowers. Savers are households, firms with surplus funds, foreigners and sometimes public bodies. Likewise borrowers can be all of these.

The foreign sector

Foreigners make a direct contribution to the economy by buying exports and selling imports. Moreover, with an increasingly interdependent world, the importance of foreign capital flows into and out of economies is growing. These capital flows play an important role alongside domestic savings in financing investment and consumer spending in economies.

Macroeconomics involves the study of the interrelationship between these five sectors and the determination of economic activity by these sectors. Inevitably, aggregation of the activities of economic agents in this way conceals information about individual behaviour. For example, a rise in the economy's total output or income tells us nothing about who receives that output or who earns the incomes. Sometimes in economic analysis it is useful to disaggregate and consider individual decision making: for instance, the individual firm's competitive strategy. In this chapter, however, we are concerned only with understanding the nature of the broad economic flows in economies. Therefore, we can make useful progress by referring to the five broad sectors above. The purpose of this chapter is to present the essence of macroeconomic activity through a simplified version of how actual economies function. The remainder of this chapter is structured as follows:

1. the measurement of economic activity, i.e. *national income accounting*;

2. problems in calculating economic activity;

3. compilation and uses of national income accounts;

4. a model of national income determination.

The measurement of economic activity

The interrelationships between the above five sectors of the economy can be summarized diagrammatically as in Figure 3.1. This diagram illustrates the flow of income and spending in an economy and is commonly referred to as the *circular flow of income model*. Although much simplified (for example, all profits are assumed to be distributed to households with none retained by firms; all taxes are imposed upon households) it does capture the essence of the macroeconomy.

The circular flow of income model represents the movement of income between households and firms and also shows the effects of the government, and the foreign and the financial sectors on this flow. It will be seen that in the case of the household sector, the extent to which the sum of households' incomes flows back to the firm sector in the form of expenditure is affected by three *leakages* – the amount saved, taxation paid to the government and the amount spent on imports. At the same time, there are three *injections* into the circular flow taking place, to some extent

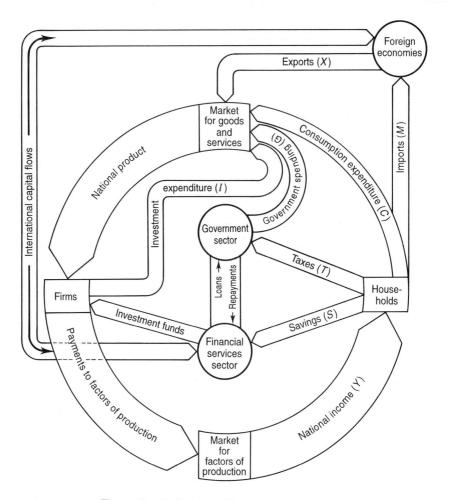

Figure 3.1 Full circular flow of income model.

offsetting the effect of these leakages. These injections are: expenditure by government on goods and services, investment expenditure by firms, and receipts from foreigners making payments for exports. The importance of these flows in the form of leakages and injections in the determination of economic activity is discussed on pages 43–9. Changes in these flows give rise to economic fluctuations and 'business cycles'. Moreover, attempts by government to influence the flows lie at the heart of macroeconomic management discussed in later chapters.

There are three methods of calculating the size of economic activity within an economy during any time period which relate to the circular flow of national income in Figure 3.1. These are the:

1. output (or production) method;
2. income method;
3. expenditure method.

Collectively, these methods of measuring the size of economic activity are referred to as *national income accounting*. In theory they should each provide the same money value for the size of economic activity because they each measure the same circular flow of income around the economy, albeit at different points in the flow. In other words, national income measured by the output method should equal national income measured by the income or expenditure methods. As the output method measures *national production*, the income method *national income* and the expenditure method *national expenditure*, it follows that:

National production = National income = National expenditure

While these equalities must always hold true in principle, in practice discrepancies (sometimes very large) arise in the collection of the relevant statistics by government. These differences arise for many reasons: errors, omissions, timing differences and so on. Perhaps the most significant omission, when the income method is used, is that relating to undeclared earnings by those people working in what is commonly referred to as the hidden or black economy. Consequently, statistical discrepancies or *residual errors* feature in national income accounts to make the three totals balance. In the UK the output total is generally believed to be a more reliable indicator of both short-term and long-term economic activity than the expenditure and income totals. Therefore, the residuals appear (though not always) in the other two totals, reflecting unmeasured expenditure and unmeasured income. Of course, these residual errors would not exist in a world of perfect statistics. Alternatively an *average* of all three totals is often used as the appropriate indicator. The importance of residual errors is diminished, however, if it can be assumed that they are relatively stable as a proportion of the total and if we are mainly concerned with changes in, rather than levels of, economic activity.

The output method

The output method calculates the total value of the final output of goods and services produced in the economy over a specified period of time. It is important to note that all final goods and services must be included regardless of whether they are sold to consumers, government, foreigners or to other firms in the form of capital equipment. To avoid the problem of double counting, and hence overestimation of the country's total output, intermediate production of goods and services must not be included in the final total. Alternatively, the problem of double counting can be avoided by summing only the *value added* by each firm at the different stages of production, rather than final outputs.

The income method

Since national income arises from the production of goods and services by the factors of production, another way of calculating the value of total output is to sum all of the incomes that these factors receive for their services – wages and salaries, rent, interest, profits and dividends. This method is referred to as the *income method* of measuring the level of economic activity in any time period. It is important to note that only incomes that have been received in return for productive services should be included. Transfer payments, therefore, must be excluded since they merely represent a redistribution of income, for instance from taxpayers to pensioners. Including these payments would lead to double counting and therefore overestimation of national income. In other words, if transfer payments were not excluded, raising pensions, unemployment benefits or similar welfare payments would lead to a statistical increase in national income when the actual (real) output of the economy had not changed.

The expenditure method

By adding up all the money values of expenditures on final goods and services produced in an economy, we arrive at the measurement of *national expenditure*. It should be noted that this will only be equal to national output if we allow for net changes in the value of the physical increase in stocks (inventories) and work in progress. Therefore, national expenditure is the sum of consumption of domestically produced goods, investment expenditure (including an allowance for changes in stocks and work in progress), expenditure by government and net receipts from foreign trade. As before, to avoid double counting, only expenditure on final goods and services should be included.

Problems in calculating economic activity

A number of problems arise when calculating the economy's total flow of national income using the above three methods. These involve:

1. allowance for capital depreciation and stock appreciation;
2. valuation of output at market prices or factor (i.e. production) cost;
3. the inclusion of net property income from abroad.

Capital depreciation and stock appreciation

During any given period some investment expenditure will merely be replacing capital, both equipment and buildings, that has worn out during the production of income and output in that period. Therefore, some allowance should be made for depreciation or capital consumption when calculating national income since this investment expenditure does not represent an increase in the economy's productive capacity or wealth. Only *net* investment (after depreciation) represents the true increase in the country's capital stock during the period. Where no allowance is made for depreciation the resulting totals are referred to as *gross* output, income or expenditure; when depreciation is deducted from the gross sum we arrive at the corresponding *net* figures. We can therefore define the following terms:

Gross national product (GNP)
Gross national expenditure (GNE) } − Depreciation
Gross national income (GNI)

$$= \begin{cases} \text{Net national product (NNP)} \\ \text{Net national expenditure (NNE)} \\ \text{Net national income (NNI)} \end{cases}$$

Estimates of depreciation are available for adjusting national income figures from gross to net. Nevertheless, when discussing national income it is common to use the gross rather than the net amounts even though the latter provide a more accurate reflection of the growth in national well-being. This is done for two reasons: because depreciation tends to change relatively slowly over time and hence gross and net figures move closely together; and because it is difficult to make an accurate estimate of depreciation at the national level. In other words, the gross figures are usually more accurate than the net figures.

Just as the government statisticians take account of depreciation or capital consumption when calculating national income figures, so they also adjust their estimates to take account of stock appreciation. It is conventional to subtract from national income totals any increase in the value of the net change in stocks of unsold goods arising from a general increase in prices. The reasoning is similar to that which lies behind adjusting for depreciation. Stock appreciation does not represent a *real* increase in a nation's output. When stock appreciation occurs it is not physical (i.e. real) output that grows, as reflected in higher stocks in the economy, it is merely that the stocks have a higher monetary (i.e. nominal) value reflecting a general rise in prices, i.e. inflation.

Market prices and factor cost

National expenditure as described above is measured initially on the basis of market (i.e. retail) prices – prices paid across the counter. These prices, however, may be distorted by the inclusion of indirect taxes and subsidies. Indirect taxes, such as VAT and excise duties, increase the prices of goods and services, while subsidies have the opposite effect. At the same time, however, national income and national product are both measured at factor cost, that is, with respect to the amounts paid to factors of production for their services excluding indirect taxes and subsidies. In order to ensure equivalence across the three methods of measuring national income, market prices must be converted to factor cost by subtracting indirect taxes and adding subsidies. Therefore we can write:

National expenditure
at factor cost   = National expenditure at market prices
                        − Indirect taxes + Subsidies

It is conventional to measure national output at factor cost rather than at market prices, otherwise any changes in indirect taxes or subsidies would distort the estimate of total output irrespective of whether there was a change in the actual quantity of goods and services produced.

Net property income from abroad

Part of an economy's measured output may have been produced by foreign-owned firms. Likewise, some domestically-owned firms may be producing output abroad. Whether we should allow for all the income resulting from these activities depends upon the purpose for which we are calculating national income. Do we wish to measure only domestic output (literally produced within the country), or do we wish to measure the output of the economy's factors of production wherever they are located? In the former case we arrive at measurements of domestic output, domestic income and domestic expenditure. In the latter case, we can allow for *net property income from abroad*. This represents the difference between the income received by the domestic economy from the production of its firms located overseas minus that income paid to overseas residents from their production in the domestic economy. For instance, profits earned by ICI abroad and remitted to the UK would be included to arrive at national production and income. Similarly, any profits earned by Nissan from producing cars in the UK and remitted to Japan would be excluded. Therefore we can write:

$$
\left.\begin{array}{l}
\text{Domestic product} \\
\text{Domestic income} \\
\text{Domestic expenditure}
\end{array}\right\}
\begin{array}{c}
\text{Net property} \\
+\ \text{income from} = \\
\text{abroad}
\end{array}
\left\{\begin{array}{l}
\text{National product} \\
\text{National income} \\
\text{National expenditure}
\end{array}\right.
$$

Table 3.1 overleaf shows a breakdown of the UK's national income accounts for 1993 based on the expenditure and income methods. Note the distinction between net and gross figures, figures at market prices and factor cost, adjustments for indirect taxes and subsidies, and the effect of net property income from abroad. Note also the existence of residual errors in the calculations using the expenditure and income methods as referred to earlier.

Compilation and uses of national income accounts

In the UK the necessary data to compile the national income accounts, using the above three methods, are collected by government departments and analyzed by government statisticians in the Central Statistical Office (CSO). The main sources of information used for the output method are the annual Census of Production and surveys by individual government departments. The income method relies largely upon information from Inland Revenue tax data together with the accounts of central and local government and public corporations. Lastly, the expenditure method is based upon figures collected from a variety of sources, such as HM Customs and Excise, Department of Trade and Industry enquiries and the Family Expenditure Survey.

National income accounts are published on an annual basis for the UK in the HMSO publication *United Kingdom National Accounts* (commonly referred to as the *Blue Book*). Apart from information at the broad aggregate level for each sector of the economy, the publication also contains detailed analyses of the various components of national income, as well as showing changes over the previous ten years. The data in this publication are of immense value to many categories of user – economists, business managers, government, international agencies and so forth (the appendix to this book lists the main sources of government statistics for the

Table 3.1 UK national income 1993.

		£m current prices
EXPENDITURE METHOD		
Consumer's expenditure		405,639
General government spending		138,224
Gross investment		94,715
Value of physical increase in stocks and work in progress		−197
Exports of goods and services	157,999	
less Imports of goods and services	−166,266	−8,267
		630,114
Statistical discrepancy (residual error)		−91
Gross domestic product at market prices (expenditure based)		630,023
Net property income from abroad		3,062
Gross national product at market prices		633,085
less Taxes on expenditure	−91,361	
plus Subsidies	7,458	−83,903
Gross national product at factor cost		549,182
less Capital consumption (depreciation)		−65,023
Net national product at factor cost		484,159
INCOME METHOD		
Income from employment		352,896
Income from self-employment		61,346
Gross trading profits of companies		73,397
Gross trading surplus of public corporations		3,415
Gross trading surplus of general government enterprises		294
Rent		52,872
Other		3,942
less Stock appreciation		−2,359
		545,803
Statistical discrepancy (residual error)		317
Gross domestic product at factor cost (income based)		546,120
Net property income from abroad		3,062
Gross national product at factor cost		549,182
less Capital consumption		−65,023
Net national product at factor cost		484,159

Source: CSO *United Kingdom National Accounts* (London: HMSO, 1994)

UK economy as well as the main international data sources). Some of the principal uses of national incomes statistics are:

1. to identify trends in consumer spending and industrial production;
2. to measure changes in the standard of living over time or to make comparisons between countries (commonly estimated in terms of national income per head);
3. to assist governments in formulating economic policies and plans;
4. to highlight changes in the distribution of national income between the factors of production (wages to labour, rent to property owners, and interest, profits, and dividends to the providers of capital).

It should be recognized that national income statistics are not perfect, especially as the sole basis for standard of living comparisons. As noted earlier, caution should always be exercised in using these statistics because of inevitable errors and omissions. Moreover, international comparisons are fraught with difficulties because of differences in conventions in the measurement and conversion of monetary values into a common unit of measurement. At the same time, the purchasing power of a common unit of currency may vary between countries. The distribution of income, provision of state welfare services, 'quality of life' and so on must also be taken into consideration when comparing average incomes per head. Ultimately, the information in national income accounts should be used alongside other indicators of economic performance and standards of living.

A model of national income determination

Equilibrium level of national income

Figure 3.1 on page 31 presented diagrammatically the interrelationships between the five main sectors of the economy. This is essentially a model showing how activity in the economy is determined in terms of a circular flow of income. We now introduce the meaning of an *equilibrium* in the national economy, based on the concepts and principles already discussed. We also consider what gives rise to *disequilibrium* in the national economy.

To illustrate the main principles consider a simple model of the circular flow of income in which there is no foreign sector (what is termed a *closed economy*) and no government intervention in the economy (see Figure 3.2). It is assumed in this figure that households either save (S) or spend on consumer goods and services (C). Firms are assumed to produce goods and services for consumption (C) and investment (I). Savings in this simplified case represent a *leakage* from the national income flow which can be counterbalanced by firms' investment expenditure, representing an

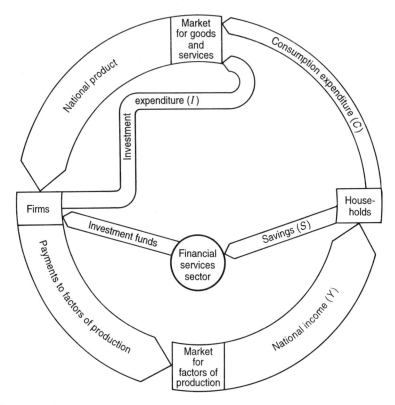

Figure 3.2 Simple model of the economy – no government sector and no foreign sector.

injection into the circular flow. Therefore, national income will be in equilibrium (i.e. its level does not change), when the value of any leakages is matched by an equal value of injections. In this simple model:

$S = I$
i.e. Leakages = Injections

This relationship, it should be stressed, applies only in this simple model of the economy. It can, however, be extended into a more general form by including the government and foreign sectors (with the financial services sector included as an intermediary). Figure 3.3, therefore, adds the government sector, while Figure 3.4 includes the foreign sector and is the same as Figure 3.1 introduced earlier.

The effect of introducing the government sector into the circular flow is that we have another leakage from the income in the form of taxation (*T*).

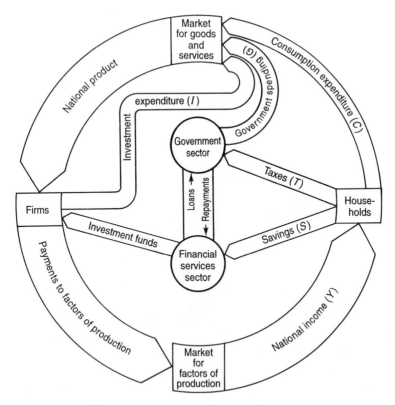

Figure 3.3 Simple model of the economy with no foreign sector.

At the same time, another injection of income arises in the form of government spending (G), as shown in Figure 3.3. Now the equilibrium condition has changed so that the economy will only be in equilibrium when

$$S + T = I + G$$
i.e. Leakages = Injections

Lastly, when the model is extended to an *open economy*, that is to say, one with foreign trade and international capital flows, a third injection into and a third leakage from the circular flow emerge. When the UK buys imports or invests overseas, the expenditure represents a leakage from the domestic economy. When foreigners buy UK exports or invest in the UK these flows represent injections of income into the UK economy. If we denote the money value of imports by M and the money value of exports by X, the general equilibrium condition for national income is now written as:

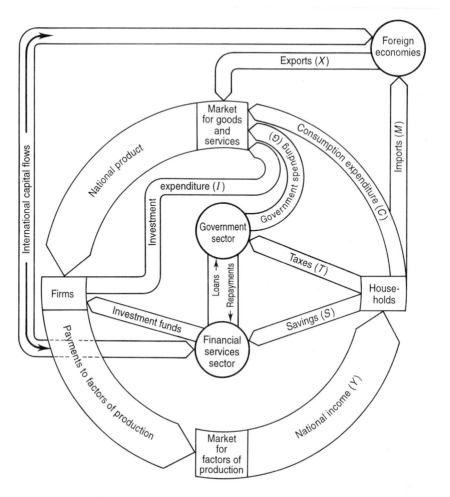

Figure 3.4 Full circular flow of income model.

$$S + T + M = I + G + X$$
i.e. Total leakages = Total injections

X and M are defined in terms of goods and services. It will be appreciated that international capital flows will be captured within the domestic expenditure flows insofar as they affect consumption and investment. On the basis of the above, we can further develop our understanding of the macroeconomy. In crude terms, equilibrium may be thought of in terms of the volume of water in a barrel. Imagine the barrel has three holes (S, T and M) and three water pipes leading into it (I, G and X) – see Figure 3.5. The level of water in the barrel will remain unchanged provided that the *total*

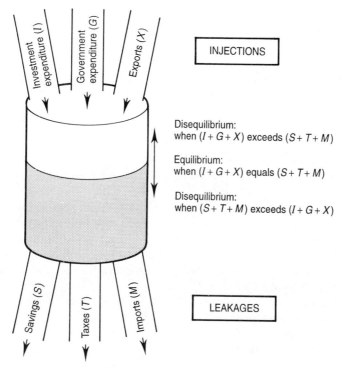

Disequilibrium:
when $(I + G + X)$ exceeds $(S + T + M)$

Equilibrium:
when $(I + G + X)$ equals $(S + T + M)$

Disequilibrium:
when $(S + T + M)$ exceeds $(I + G + X)$

Figure 3.5 National income equilibrium – leakages and injections.

volume of water leaking from the barrel is matched by the *total* amount flowing into it. When the total outflow equals the total inflow, the water level remains in equilibrium or balance.

An equivalent way of expressing equilibrium, but this time for an economy's national income rather than the water level in a barrel, is in terms of aggregate demand for and aggregate supply of goods and services. The equilibrium level of national income exists in an economy when:

Aggregate demand (AD) = Aggregate supply (AS)

Only when this condition is met can we state that the total value of domestic goods and services that households, government, firms and foreigners want to buy is matched by the total value of goods and services firms want to supply. Note that this refers to the demand for and supply of *domestic* goods and services (that is, including the value of exports and after deduction of expenditure on imports).

It should be appreciated that aggregate supply represents the amount of goods and services that firms are willing to produce, given the general level of wages and prices. Hence, an equilibrium national income relates to the situation where the production *plans* of firms match the *actual* supply of goods and services needed to satisfy aggregate demand in a particular time period. When this condition is satisfied there is no tendency for the economy to move away from equilibrium.

From this discussion of equilibrium it is easy to understand the meaning of a disequilibrium level of national income.

Disequilibrium level of national income

Refer back to Figure 3.5. Obviously, if the total leakage $(S + T + M)$ exceeds the total injection $(I + G + X)$, the water level will be falling. Conversely, if the total injection exceeds the total leakage then the water level must be rising. Both situations represent disequilibria since the level of water in the barrel is not constant. The same principle applies to an economy's national income. In summary, therefore, a disequilibrium level of national income occurs when the total value of leakages is greater than or less than the total value of injections, i.e.:

$(S + T + M)$ is greater than $(I + G + X)$
            or
$(S + T + M)$ is less than $(I + G + X)$

or, equivalently, in terms of AD and AS

AD is less than or greater than AS

When national income is at equilibrium, there will be no tendency for prices in general to rise due to excess demand since total demand is matched by the total supply of goods and services. In addition, there will be no tendency for unemployment to rise owing to inadequate demand for the available supply of goods and services. However, in reality, economies are rarely if ever in situations of stable prices and employment levels because savings (and therefore consumer spending), taxes, investment expenditure, government expenditure, exports and imports, are all changing continuously. The real world is dominated by disequilibrium situations with rising and falling prices (inflation and deflation) and changes in the level of employment and hence unemployment.

Many economists would argue that the role of government should be to manage the macroeconomy by influencing the levels of injections and leakages and hence the degree and direction of economic activity. This may be carried out using a range of policy measures focusing upon either the demand side of the economy (adjusting the level of aggregate demand) –

the level of water in the barrel – or the supply side of the economy (affecting the total output of the economy) – the size of the barrel! This gives rise to *demand management* policies and *supply-side* policies detailed in later chapters. A controversial issue in policy making today is the extent to which governments should emphasize either demand-side or supply-side measures in influencing the level of economic activity.

Concluding remarks

In this chapter we have discussed how national income – economic activity – is measured by the output, income and expenditure methods. We have seen that whichever method is used, the resulting totals should be identical because each method measures the same economic activity, albeit at different points in the circular flow around the economy. By focusing upon the circular flow of national income we were then able to identify certain injections into the economy and certain leakages out of it – the injections being investment, government expenditure and export revenues, and the leakages savings, taxation and import expenditure. When injections exceed leakages, like the rising water level in a barrel when more water flows in than out, the total income flowing around the economy increases. In other words, the level of economic activity rises. Conversely, when the leakages from the income flow exceed the injections into it, the level of income, and therefore the level of economic activity, falls.

Just as imbalances between the injections into and the leakages from the circular flow of income lead to changes in the level of economic activity, so it follows that an equilibrium in the level of national income will occur when the total value of injections *equals* the total value of leakages. An alternative way of looking at this is to say that an equilibrium national income level occurs when aggregate demand equals aggregate supply.

In the next chapter we develop this analysis further, initially by looking in more detail at the different components of aggregate demand and then by discussing the impact of changes in aggregate demand upon the equilibrium level of national income.

4

National income
determination

The essence of national income determination

In Chapter 3 we illustrated the flows of outputs, incomes and expenditures around an economy in the form of the circular flow of income model, which is a useful diagrammatic summary of economic activity. We now turn to discuss the determination of these flows, i.e. the underlying dynamics of the macroeconomy. We are essentially interested in understanding what *causes* the level of national income to rise or fall in the short term around an economy's long-term growth path. Such fluctuations in national income give rise to what are known as *business cycles* in which the rate of growth in production periodically rises and falls.

This chapter considers the causes of fluctuations in national income and therefore employment and prices employing a framework developed by Keynesian economists. This forms a basis for the study of fiscal and monetary policies in the following chapters.

Keynesians versus monetarists: an overview

Views on what determines national income may be broadly divided into two schools of thought: the Keynesian and the monetarist (though it could be argued that most economists today hold views drawn from both schools).

The Keynesian view

This view has evolved from the work of the Cambridge economist John Maynard Keynes, as set out in his book *The General Theory of Employment, Interest and Money* (1936). His ideas had a profound impact upon economists and governments in the post-war period and led to the concept of *Keynesian demand management*. Keynes and his followers argued that the levels of total output (aggregate supply) and employment in an economy are determined by the level of aggregate demand for goods and services. Their views were concerned largely with short-run measures to affect the level of economic activity focusing on changes in demand. Today, economists who incline towards a Keynesian approach to the economy still believe that when an economy has spare productive capacity and unemployment, investment and output can be stimulated so as to increase employment without creating inflationary pressure. They argue that this can be achieved primarily through changing government expenditure and/ or taxes – that is, by what are known as *fiscal policy* measures (fiscal policy is discussed in detail in the next chapter).

The monetarist view

This view came to prominence during the early 1970s following the apparent failure of Keynesian demand management policies to bring down inflation and reduce unemployment. The monetarist approach stems largely from the work of the American economist Milton Friedman. Based partly on empirical research, initially into the historical relationship between the growth in the money supply and inflation in the USA, and partly on a theoretical study of the relationship between money supply and money GDP (the value of domestic output), Friedman argued that controlling the growth of the money supply is necessary to bring down inflation. Monetarist economists also argue that controlling inflation is a prerequisite to reducing unemployment since inflation in market econom- ies, they believe, is harmful to private business and therefore economic growth.

Monetarist policy prescriptions, like Keynesian policy prescriptions, are directed at aggregate demand in the economy (for an alternative approach which focuses upon increasing the capacity of the economy to supply goods and services competitively – i.e. supply-side economics – see Chapter 7). However, unlike Keynesians, monetarists tend to eschew positive state action to increase employment, especially through the use of fiscal measures. Instead, they prefer to rely upon private investment and free markets. Insofar as government has a role to play in the economy, monetarists argue that it is to provide an environment conducive to private enterprise, including the maintenance of private property rights, establishing a framework of law which maximizes individual freedom, and controlling the growth in the money supply to prevent inflation and unexpected fluctuations in aggregate demand. Monetary policy measures are discussed in detail in Chapter 6.

The components of aggregate demand

The starting point for an analysis of fluctuations in national income is the concept of an equilibrium national income as introduced in the previous chapter. By the term equilibrium, economists mean a state of affairs in which the forces that are influencing change in opposite directions are perfectly balanced so that there is no tendency to change. Therefore, a national income equilibrium occurs when the demand for goods and services in the economy is just equal to the supply of goods and services available for purchase. There is then no tendency for the national income to rise or fall. If demand exceeds the output of goods and services, however, either output or prices, or both, will tend to rise, leading to a higher nominal value of national income. A rise in the *nominal* value of national income does not necessarily mean that the *real* value will rise: this will depend upon the economy's ability to increase output at a faster rate than any rise in prices. Similarly, if output exceeds demand either prices or output, or both, will tend to fall, leading to a decline in the nominal value of national income. Again, the real value of national income will depend upon the relative changes in output and prices. In other words, a national income equilibrium occurs when:

Aggregate supply = Aggregate demand

Aggregate supply is the total output of the economy (i.e. national income) and is commonly denoted by the letter Y. Aggregate demand is made up of a number of components as we saw in the circular flow diagrams in Chapter 3. These are consumer spending (C), investment expenditure (I), government spending (G) and exports (X). Of course, in order to calculate the demand for domestically produced goods and services, we must subtract expenditure on imports (M) since the goods bought by domestic households, firms and government are likely to include a foreign component (e.g. imported raw materials). Therefore, the equilibrium condition can be expressed as:

$$Y = C + I + G + (X - M)$$

In order to understand how changes in national income (Y) may be determined by changes in aggregate demand, we must examine each of the components of aggregate demand in turn.

Consumer spending and savings

Domestic consumer spending is the dominant component of aggregate demand in all economies, dwarfing the other expenditures. For example, around two-thirds of the UK's total domestic expenditure is accounted for by consumption. Therefore, any changes in consumption are likely to have a significant impact upon the level of economic activity in an economy. More spending in the High Street raises aggregate demand, while a fall in consumer confidence will deflate domestic spending, with obvious implications for firms' sales and production. Since consumers can spend or save their income, it follows that for any given post-tax income level, when the percentage of income spent on consumer goods and services rises, the level of savings falls. In contrast, a decline in the share of post-tax income spent on consumption raises the percentage of income saved.

In addition to income, a number of other factors may affect consumption, such as consumer confidence, the wealth of consumers (as reflected in savings, etc.), the availability of credit, government taxation and subsidies, advertising of goods and services and so on. Nevertheless, economists tend to single out *disposable income* as the most important influence. Disposable income (Y_d) is the amount of income that consumers have left over after paying direct taxes to the government and receiving direct state subsidies, e.g. child benefit. One way of expressing the relationship between consumer spending and disposable income is to say that an individual's total consumption (C) is dependent upon (or, to use the mathematical term, a function of – denoted by the letter f) disposable income. This is written as:

$$C = f(Y_d)$$

It also follows that as disposable income can be spent or saved, savings (S) are also a function of disposable income, i.e.:

$$S = f(Y_d)$$

The proportion of disposable income that goes towards consumer spending is referred to as the *average propensity to consume (apc)*. In notation form:

$$apc = \frac{\text{Total consumption expenditure}}{\text{Total disposable income}} = C/Y_d$$

Similarly, the proportion of disposable income saved is known as the *average propensity to save (aps)*. In notation form:

$$aps = \frac{\text{Total savings}}{\text{Total disposable income}} = S/Y_d$$

By definition, the numerical values of the average propensities to consume and save must sum to 1 since household disposable income is either spent (consumed) or saved, i.e.:

$$apc + aps = 1$$

When total disposable income rises in an economy, and since consumption and savings are related to income, total consumer spending and savings will also increase. Similarly, when total disposable income falls, spending and savings will decline. The proportion of any increase in disposable income which is spent on consumer goods and services is known as the *marginal propensity to consume (mpc)*, while that part of any increase which is absorbed by extra savings is referred to as the *marginal propensity to save (mps)*. More formally:

$$mpc = \frac{\text{Change in consumption expenditure}}{\text{Change in disposable income}} = \Delta C/\Delta Y_d$$

$$mps = \frac{\text{Change in savings}}{\text{Change in disposable income}} = \Delta S/\Delta Y_d$$

where Δ is a shorthand notation for 'a small change in' or increment.

Once again, since household disposable income can only be used for consumption or savings, it follows that the numerical values of the marginal propensities to consume and save must sum to 1, i.e.:

$$mpc + mps = 1$$

An example might help to clarify the meaning of the terms *apc*, *aps*, *mpc* and *mps*. Suppose, for instance, that an individual household spends 72 per cent of its total disposable income of £500 on consumer goods (i.e. C = £360) and saves the rest (S = £140). If the household's disposable income now rises to £600, it might decide to spend £60 of the extra £100, saving the remainder. Initially, the *apc* was 0.72 (i.e. £360/£500) and the *aps* 0.28 (i.e. £140/£500) but now the *apc* is 0.7 (i.e. £420/£600) and the *aps* is 0.3

(i.e. £180/£600). The *mpc* and *mps* can also be calculated. The *mpc* is 0.6 (= £60/£100) and the *mps* 0.4 (= £40/£100).

This example illustrates a tendency that Keynes believed affected all economies: over the long term, as disposable incomes rise, people tend to save a larger proportion of any increase in income (note that although this may not be true for all individuals, all that is being argued is that it will tend to be true for the economy as a whole). In other words, the *mpc*, and therefore the *apc*, tend to fall. By similar logic we can deduce that different income groups in society at any given time can be expected to have different propensities to consume and save. In general, we would expect richer social groups to save a larger percentage of any increase in disposable income than poorer groups.

The magnitudes of the propensities to consume and save will, of course, be influenced over time by a number of factors such as changes in the distribution of income (the impact of taxes and state welfare payments), the availability of credit, interest paid on savings, and the age distribution of the population (the young and the retired tend to spend a large proportion of their incomes on consumption, whereas middle-aged people usually have a higher propensity to save).

Many economists question whether consumption and savings are directly linked to current disposable incomes. Consumption and savings may not react immediately to changes in income. For instance, people may draw on past savings to maintain consumption when current disposable incomes fall, say in the early stages of an economic recession, particularly if they believe that their incomes will subsequently recover. This leads to the idea that consumption is dependent upon people's perceptions of their *permanent* incomes rather than their current disposable incomes. If this is the case, consumption may not react immediately to changes in income during cyclical fluctuations in economy activity. In economic upturns consumption will tend to lag behind the rise in income, while in economic downturns the rate of consumption will not fall as quickly as the fall in the growth rate of incomes. An alternative approach relates current consumption to some perception of *lifetime* incomes. For example, a young trainee professional may spend at a relatively high rate anticipating a larger income later in her career. The exact nature of the relationship between consumption and current income continues to be researched. Nevertheless, current income is usually a significant influence on consumption. Hence, to assume that consumption is dependent simply upon current disposable income and that the *mpc* falls or stays constant as incomes rise is satisfactory for the overview of national income determination that we are developing in this chapter.

The relationship between total consumer expenditure and national income can be shown diagrammatically – see Figure 4.1. This relationship is known as the *consumption function* and plays an important role in

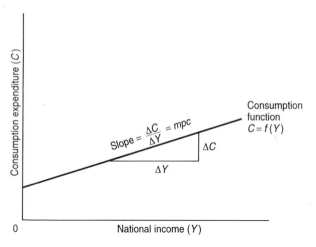

Figure 4.1 The consumption function.

Keynesian economics. It will be noted that, for simplicity, we have assumed that consumption (and hence savings) has a constant relationship with national income and is thus shown as a straight line (the *mpc* is therefore assumed to be constant given by the slope of the consumption function). We have also assumed that there is no direct taxation, i.e. that C is related to total income instead of disposable income. This is a common assumption used merely to simplify the analysis.

Investment expenditure

Private investment is another major component of aggregate demand. The relationship between investment expenditure and national income, however, is far more complex than the relationship between consumption expenditure and national income. In practice, investment expenditure decisions by firms in the private sector are likely to be dependent upon a host of factors such as interest rates, return on capital, technology, the growth in consumer demand, taxation and investment incentives, business confidence and expectations, as well as the level of and changes in national income itself. Given this complexity, it does not seem unreasonable to argue, as many economists have done as a simplifying assumption, that investment (*I*) is largely *independent* of the level of national income. In Keynesian analysis of economic fluctuations, in particular, the emphasis tends to be more upon the effects on investment of changes in business confidence than changes in national income as such.

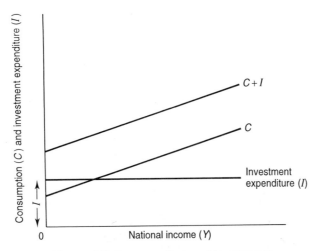

Figure 4.2 Consumption and investment.

If investment is treated as being independent of national income levels then we can illustrate this by graphing the level of investment as a straight line parallel to the national income axis as in Figure 4.2. The amount of investment, I, is determined by the other possible factors affecting investment already referred to, such that when any of these change, investment rises or falls as appropriate: i.e. the investment line shifts up or down. Moreover, if we add the actual amount of investment in the economy, I, to the consumption function as shown in Figure 4.1, we can derive a C + I line as illustrated in Figure 4.2.

Government expenditure

In the UK the third component of aggregate demand, government expenditure on final consumption and investment, (G), currently accounts for over a fifth of total final expenditure (excluding transfer payments such as social security benefits – see Chapter 3, page 42). Despite a Conservative government in the 1980s elected to reduce public spending, current expenditure in particular continued to rise (e.g. on social security payments including pensions) through that decade, while expenditure on capital account (e.g. public buildings and roads) was more tightly controlled.

Government current and capital spending, like investment, is affected by many factors (in this case political and social as well as economic) and, like investment, it is difficult to predict a stable and reliable relationship

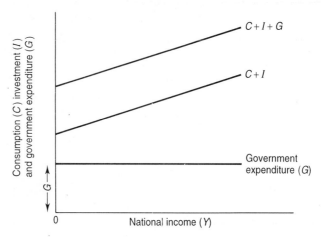

Figure 4.3 Consumption, investment and government expenditure.

between national income and government expenditure. For example, the introduction of a new road-building or school-building programme is much more likely to be influenced by traffic density and the numbers of schoolchildren than national income. It is not clear either what will happen to government spending when national income fluctuates. For instance, when the national income falls, governments might attempt to rein back their spending so as to avoid a rise in the tax burden. On the other hand, economic recessions lead to higher unemployment and more social deprivation, which tend to increase public spending.

Given the uncertainty about how government spending will change as national income changes, we shall assume that G, like investment, is independent of national income, at least for the sake of illustration. It is therefore shown as a horizontal line in Figure 4.3, with G representing the total value of government spending. Should government expenditure rise or fall for whatever reason, unrelated to a change in national income, this will be reflected in the diagram by a parallel shift upwards or downwards in the line. Moreover, adding G to C and I gives the line $C + I + G$ as shown in Figure 4.3.

Export and import expenditure

We can now complete our analysis of aggregate demand by adding the difference between expenditure on exports (X) and imports (M) to $C + I + G$. When foreigners buy our exports, take holidays in our country or travel using our national airline for example, the amount remitted to our economy becomes part of the total demand for our goods and services. Similarly, when we buy foreign goods, take holidays abroad and use foreign airlines, for example, income leaks out of our circular flow of income (in the way explained in Chapter 3) and is lost to our economy (except that these funds in turn permit people in other countries to buy our exports, see Chapter 8). In the same way, any flows of funds into the country for investment purposes, including investments in stocks and shares, bank accounts and more tangible investments such as the building of new offices and factories, add to demand here by boosting consumption (C) and investment (I). In contrast, when residents of our economy invest overseas this takes funds out of the country, thereby adding to demand abroad but reducing it here.

We shall assume for convenience that X and M, like I and G, are independent of national income, although this is a gross simplification. Export levels for goods and services are usually more related to the level of incomes in export markets than domestic national income, but booming demand at home may lead to potential exports being diverted to the home market, producing an inverse relationship between domestic national income and exports. Turning to imports, we tend to buy more imported goods and services as our incomes rise. In general, although exports and imports may be affected by changes in national income, the precise relationship is quite complex. Rather than pursue this further we shall assume that X and M are independent of national income. Once again, such a simplifying assumption allows us to make progress without detracting from the significance of the discussion.

The difference between X and M can be positive or negative depending upon whether the value of exports is greater or less than the value of imports. Assuming that it is positive, adding $X - M$ to C, I and G gives the aggregate demand schedule as shown in Figure 4.4, illustrating the relationship between total expenditure in the economy and national income. In this figure the vertical distance between the lines $C + I + G$ (as derived above) and $C + I + G + (X - M)$ represents the resulting net value of exports and imports. Therefore, if imports were greater than exports, the $C + I + G + (X - M)$ line would lie below the $C + I + G$ line.

Deflationary and inflationary gaps

Having considered each category of aggregate demand and its relationship to national income, we can now develop Keynesian analysis further and, in particular, look at the circumstances in which an equilibrium national income equates with unemployment or inflation. It will be recalled from the above discussion and Chapter 3 that equilibrium in an economy exists

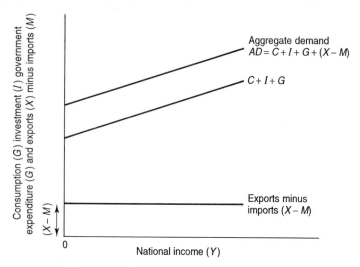

Figure 4.4 Aggregate demand schedule.

when aggregate demand equals aggregate supply so that there are no forces making for a change in national income. We have shown that aggregate demand (AD) is given by $C + I + G + (X - M)$ and that aggregate supply represents the total output of the economy and is therefore the same as the national income (Y). Therefore, as a condition of equilibrium we can write:

$$Y = AD = C + I + G + (X - M)$$

If values of Y and AD are graphed together, then equilibrium positions of the economy will be shown along a 45° line (assuming the same scales are used on both axes) (see Figure 4.5). In other words, any point along this 45° line represents an equality between the level of national income (i.e. output or aggregate supply) and the level of aggregate demand.

Superimposing the aggregate demand schedule in Figure 4.4 onto this diagram allows us to identify what level of equilibrium activity in the economy exists at any particular point in time. This is shown in Figure 4.6, where the equilibrium national income is at Y_e. This is the only level of aggregate demand where the economy is in equilibrium. Movement towards other levels of aggregate demand would lead to a rise or fall in national income. For example, point A on the aggregate demand line indicates an aggregate demand greater than aggregate supply and is therefore not an equilibrium point. Similarly, point B indicates an aggregate demand which is less than the aggregate supply. Again, this cannot represent an equilibrium level of national income. Remember that

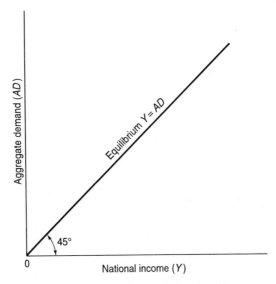

Figure 4.5 Equilibrium level of national income.

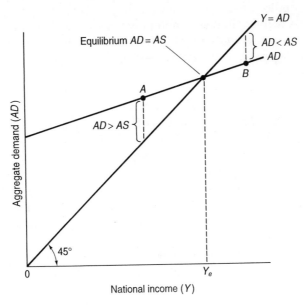

Figure 4.6 Aggregate demand and equilibrium level of national income.

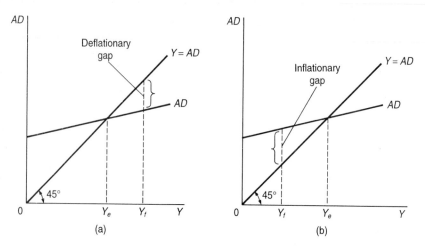

Figure 4.7 (a) Deflationary and (b) inflationary gaps.

while the line *AD* shows all the levels of aggregate demand in relation to different national income levels, only where *AD* = *AS* can there be an equilibrium level of national income and this must be where the *AD* line crosses the 45° line – the 45° line having been drawn to show all equilibrium points where *AD* = *AS*.

Using this type of analysis it is easy to show how the economy could be stable or in equilibrium either at low or high levels of economic activity. Low economic activity implies unemployment of the nation's resources, while high economic activity implies that the economy is operating near to or at full employment. This gives rise to the notion of *deflationary* and *inflationary gaps* respectively.

Deflationary and inflationary gaps

A deflationary gap is the amount by which aggregate demand must be increased to raise the equilibrium level of national income (Y_e) to its full employment level (Y_f). Conversely, an inflationary gap shows the amount by which *AD* must be decreased in order to bring the equilibrium income down from Y_e to Y_f with stable prices. Both of these possibilities are shown in Figure 4.7. In the case of Figure 4.7(a), the equilibrium level of national income is to the left of that level which would ensure full employment of resources (Y_f). Aggregate demand is less than the country's potential output would be if all resources were fully employed. The economy is therefore suffering from unemployment of people and other resources because of a deficiency in demand, and this may also mean that prices are falling. This situation is similar to that which faced the UK economy in the early 1930s and which so influenced Keynes when he propounded his theory on the cause of general unemployment in 1936. According to Keynes, the problem lay with insufficient aggregate demand to generate enough economic activity to provide full employment. In other words, the economy was suffering from a deflationary gap between the existing level of aggregate demand and the full employment supply of goods and services. His policy prescription at that time, therefore, was that the economy should 'spend, spend, spend' its way out of recession. As it proved difficult to encourage the private sector to spend, it was proposed that the lead should be taken by the government – hence the growth in significance of fiscal policy as a demand management tool (see Chapter 5).

In the case of Figure 4.7(b), the equilibrium national income is to the right of the full employment level. That is to say, the level of aggregate demand exceeds the value of output at full employment with stable prices. Since, to be in equilibrium income level aggregate demand must equal aggregate supply, what is going on? The answer lies in rising prices (inflation). The economy is at the full employment level of output but excess demand, equal to the inflationary gap, is pushing up the general level of prices. This means that there is demand for goods and services that has been satisfied only by raising prices.

Neither deflationary nor inflationary gaps are desirable, so an obvious further question is how these gaps can be closed so as to achieve full employment with stable prices. In answering this question there is a division amongst economists and policy makers. Indeed, this question arguably raises the biggest controversy in macroeconomics today: the necessary degree of state intervention in the management of the economy.

On the one hand, free market economists (who are often monetarists, although by no means all monetarists are passionate about the free market) argue that private enterprise in conjunction with competitive markets will eventually restore an equilibrium level of national income with full employment and low or zero inflation. The free market is self-regulating, therefore state intervention is at best unnecessary and at worst hampers the operation of market forces. On the other hand, Keynesians (incidentally along with other groups, notably Marxist economists, whose views are not explored in this book) dispute that the market economy can be relied upon to adjust to full employment with stable prices. Either the process will not occur at all or, if it does, it will take too long and have unacceptable social and political consequences. Writing at a time of protracted unemployment, Keynes dismissed the idea of waiting for market adjustments, observing succinctly: 'in the long run we are all dead'.

Adopting a Keynesian stance (we consider monetarist and free market views in more detail in Chapters 6 and 7), if free market forces are not capable of regulating the level of economic activity, then there is a clear case for state intervention. This leads to a subsidiary question concerning how governments might attempt to influence economic activity in order to close deflationary and inflationary gaps in aggregate demand. In other words, how can aggregate demand be changed in an economy to reverse deflationary pressures or to squeeze out inflationary pressures?

Keynesian economists assign the responsibility for managing aggregate demand to government, using *fiscal policy* measures especially, which may involve either or both of the following:

1. Changes in personal taxation to influence consumer spending and therefore aggregate demand.
2. Changes in government spending, again to influence aggregate demand directly.

In addition to using fiscal policy to influence consumption and change government spending, other possibilities recognized by Keynesians involve affecting the level of private investment and the flow of exports and imports. For example, since 1945 various governments under the influence of Keynesian precepts have introduced investment incentives, changed interest rates in a countercyclical fashion, offered export induce-ments from time to time, and have resorted to import controls of various kinds to limit spending on imports (such attempts by governments to moderate economic activity in the post-war period in a Keynesian fashion were known as 'stop–go' or fine-tuning policies).

Keynesian economists stress that initial changes in investment, govern-ment spending and export and import revenues have a multiple impact upon changes in national income and that this effect can be broadly estimated. This gives rise to one of the most important concepts in Keynesian macroeconomic analysis with regard to the measurement of the impact of changes in aggregate demand, namely the *multiplier*.

Measuring the impact of changes in aggregate demand: the multiplier

Changes in any of the components of aggregate demand will have an effect on the equilibrium level of national income (Y_e). For example, a change in any of the injections into or leakages from the circular flow of income will bring about a change in the level of Y. As we have already discussed, injections refer to either government spending (G), investment spending (I) or export revenues (X), which add to the circular flow; while leakages refer to taxation (T), savings (S) or expenditure on imports (M), which reduce the amount of income circulating around the economy.

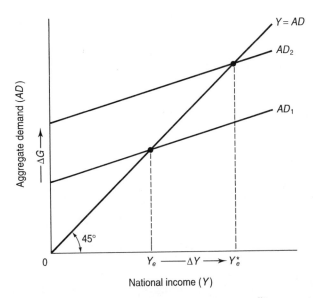

Figure 4.8 The impact of increasing government expenditure upon aggregate demand.

Let us consider a change in one of the injections. For example, if the government decides to raise its level of expenditure then, by definition, aggregate demand in the economy will increase, as shown in Figure 4.8. The increase in G is depicted as a vertical movement in aggregate demand from AD_1 to AD_2. Therefore, an initial increase in government expenditure has given rise to a new equilibrium level of national income Y_e^*. It is important to notice, however, that the initial increase in government expenditure is less than the consequent increase in national income. This is a fundamental point of Keynesian analysis. In general, an initial increase in aggregate demand leads to a larger total increase in national income. The extent to which Y changes as a result of a change in an injection or leakage is measured by the *national income multiplier*.

The multiplier effect is defined as *the ratio of the resultant change in national income to the initial change in injections or leakages*. This gives rise to measures such as the government expenditure multiplier ($\Delta Y/\Delta G$), investment multiplier ($\Delta Y/\Delta I$) and the export multiplier ($\Delta Y/\Delta X$), where, as before, Δ means 'change in' or increment. Similarly, we can measure the multiplier effects of changes in any of the leakages, i.e. $\Delta Y/\Delta T$, $\Delta Y/\Delta S$ and $\Delta Y/\Delta M$. In more general terms:

$$\text{Size of the multiplier} = \frac{\text{Change in national income}}{\text{Initial change in aggregate demand}}$$

From Figure 4.8 it should be clear that the value of the multiplier is dependent upon the slope of the aggregate demand line. In our simplified example, this slope is equal to the marginal propensity to consume (*mpc*) since the other components of aggregate demand (*G*, *I* and *X*−*M*) have been assumed to be unrelated to national income. In this simple case, therefore, the impact of any change in aggregate demand will depend upon the size of the leakage from the circular flow of income in the form of savings. That is, the multiplier will depend upon the *mps* and may be measured as:

Multiplier = 1/*mps*

This is equivalent to $1/(1 - mpc)$ since the *mpc* + *mps* = 1 (as noted on page 54). However, in addition to savings, the other two leakages from the circular flow (taxation and expenditure on imports) generally affect the size of the multiplier. In this case the formula for the multiplier is a little more complicated, being defined as:

Multiplier = 1/(*mps* + *mpt* + *mpm*)

where *mps* is the marginal propensity to save, $\Delta S/\Delta Y$; *mpt* the marginal propensity to pay taxes, $\Delta T/\Delta Y$; and *mpm* the marginal propensity to import, $\Delta M/\Delta Y$.

A 'demultiplier' effect will also arise when we have a reduction in any of the injections *I*, *G* and *X*. A reduction in aggregate demand will lead to a multiplied reduction in national income.

Recalling the circular flow of income model, summarized diagrammatically in Figure 3.1, we can visualize an initial addition to aggregate demand going around the economy; but as it does so some of the additional spending is lost to the circular flow because it leaks out through savings, expenditure on imported goods and services, and to the government in the form of taxation. In other words, the amount of extra spending circulating around the economy for a second time is smaller (than that which was injected initially) by the amount which leaked out in the first round. Similarly, the amount circulating in the third round is less than that which circulated in the second by the amount which leaked out in the second round, and so on. Therefore, the amount of additional expenditure circulating around the economy declines continuously until it becomes negligible. If we added up the amount of extra demand or income generated in each round we should find that it is a multiple of the initial injection – this multiple being smaller the larger the leakages from the circular flow in the form of savings, spending on imports and taxation. The total increase in income in relation to the initial increase in expenditure is the multiplier. So that, for instance, if total income rises by twice the initial expenditure then the multiplier has a value of two.

The multiplier effect is often likened to throwing a stone into the centre of a lake, causing ripples which spread throughout the water. The ripples are greatest at the centre but diminish nearer the banks. This gives rise to the notion of 'regional' as well as national multiplier effects with the leakage of income into imports now defined as spending outside of the region in question. For example, a new government shipbuilding order for Barrow-in-Furness would probably have its greatest impact upon national income in the surrounding area, especially in terms of increased employment and therefore expenditure in local shops and clubs. However, other areas further afield would also benefit from new shipyard orders and the increased spending power of the shipyard workers. The larger the spending on goods and services outside the Barrow-in-Furness area the smaller the regional multiplier effect of the new shipbuilding order. Since 'imports' include all spending outside of the region, generally the smaller the region, the smaller the multiplier. For this reason, national income multipliers can be expected to be larger than regional income multipliers.

The importance of the national income multiplier

The analysis so far may seem somewhat remote from the real world of business managers. Diagrams with 45° lines, consumption functions, equilibrium national incomes and national income multipliers are not part of the normal vocabulary of business; nor do they appear often in press reporting of economic events. However, they are important concepts if we are really to understand how an economy functions. It is one thing, for example, to read in the financial columns that the rate of growth of the economy is falling, it is quite another to appreciate the full significance of this – both in terms of why it is declining and the implications for business. In particular, changes in aggregate demand have direct and powerful effects on the business sector in terms of output and profits, aggravated by the multiplier effect. A sound understanding and awareness of likely changes in economic activity is essential if firms are to plan their production levels and their marketing strategies successfully.

In addition, many industries are affected directly by private and public sector investment programmes, both local and national. In this context, an appreciation of multiplier effects is of immense value in helping to plan ahead. For example, decisions by the government to build new roads have a significant impact upon directly related industrial sectors such as the various construction industries. But there are also likely to be important knock-on effects from large investment programmes for the rest of the economy. A recent example was the building of the Channel Tunnel which had far-reaching effects on employment levels and output throughout the whole of the UK, and especially with regard to the local economy in the south-east.

Not only can businesses gain from an understanding of the multiplier process, it also provides a simple but useful quantitative guide for the government in assessing the impact of policy measures upon the economy. Government economic policies may even be directed at influencing the size of the multiplier itself, and hence aggregate demand, through effecting changes in the rate of taxation, the level of savings and the flow of imports.

Governments usually resort to demand management when the economy is in danger of 'overheating', that is, when domestic demand exceeds the ability of the economy to supply goods and services, thereby aggravating inflation and attracting imports. Similarly, in the case of downturns in economic activity, the government may decide to intervene and stimulate aggregate demand to boost output. In both cases, in deciding by how much demand should be lowered or raised in order to reduce or increase national income to the desired level, account must be taken of the multiplier effects. For example, if the government estimates that demand must decline by £4bn to bring down inflation, and the multiplier effect of government spending is estimated to be two, then government spending needs only to be reduced by £2bn for the target to be achieved. Indeed, if government spending was reduced by the full £4bn and the multiplier remained at two, the result would be a severe and unintended collapse in aggregate demand and national income of £8bn.

The use of Keynesian demand management policies is further illustrated below with respect to *business cycles*. In order to appreciate this topic more fully, however, we shall first introduce another important economic concept concerning the impact of changes in expenditure upon national income, known as the accelerator principle.

The accelerator principle

The accelerator principle relates to *changes* in the level of investment in an economy and, more specifically, to the impact of changes in consumption upon investment. A small increase in the output of consumer goods and services tends to lead to a larger increase in the production of capital equipment needed to produce those goods. This change in output in the capital goods industry then has an impact upon the economy by accelerating the pace of growth – hence the name. The accelerator can also work in reverse. A small decline in demand for consumer goods and services tends to lead to the shelving of investment plans, which in turn provokes a fall in orders for capital equipment and ultimately a downturn in the rate of economic growth.

A brief example might help to clarify the accelerator principle. Suppose that a firm manufactures goods using ten machines, each of which produces 1,000 units per annum. Also suppose that the total demand for the firm's output is currently 10,000 units per annum. To simplify the discussion we will assume no depreciation, therefore all investment expands capacity. Now, if demand remained at 10,000 units per annum, no investment would take place; but if demand rose to, say, 12,000 units then two new machines would be ordered to produce the extra output. If subsequently demand rose again, this time to 15,000 units, a further three machines would be purchased and so forth. Note that the 3,000 rise in demand represents a 25 per cent increase in the output of goods (i.e. from 12,000 to 15,000 units that year) while the three extra machines amount to a 50 per cent rise in the production of the machine manufacturing industry (i.e. from two to three machines that year). Hence the rise in consumer demand has caused an accelerated increase in the demand for new machines. Equally, of course, if at some stage demand ceased to grow then the firm would cease investing and again a small fall in consumer demand would trigger a much larger proportionate fall in the demand for machines.

This process by which investment jumps as consumer demand rises and then collapses when the growth in demand ends can be observed in all economies and makes the state of new orders for the engineering industry a good barometer of changes in the overall level of economic activity. Specifically, the accelerator principle highlights the following:

1. Net investment by a firm will be maintained only if the demand for the firm's output continues to rise at a steady rate.

2. Demand for consumer goods and services must increase *at an increasing rate* if net investment is to rise.

3. When demand ceases to grow then net investment becomes zero.

In practice, the accelerator principle does not work quite so mechanically as set out above. In particular, investment decisions are also affected by business expectations: for example, businesses may continue to invest during a downturn in consumer demand if they feel it is temporary and that investment is necessary if they are to compete successfully in the future. Similarly, if a firm is working with excess capacity, an increase in consumer demand might be met out of this excess capacity rather than through new investment. Nevertheless, the accelerator effect operates in economies, albeit in a crude way, and is important in an understanding of the causes of economic fluctuations. More particularly, the accelerator emphasizes the interrelationships between income, consumer demand, investment and the business cycle. Since a change in consumer demand is largely dependent upon a change in national income (Y) from one time period to the next, and investment (I) is affected by changes in consumer demand, the accelerator principle in its most simple form can be expressed as:

$$I = a\Delta Y$$

where I is current net investment expenditure or fixed capital, a the accelerator effect, and ΔY the change in national income or output between the current and previous time period. In other words, the level of investment is related to changes in income over time by the accelerator process.

The business cycle

The business (or trade) cycle is the term used by economists to describe the continual ups and downs in the rate of growth of national income experienced since the Industrial Revolution. Economists in the nineteenth century first became aware of fairly regular cycles of economic activity in industrial economies, many lasting between seven and ten years – although the precise length of cycles has proven as controversial as the different explanations that have been put forward as to their cause. The English economist William Stanley Jevons propounded in the 1870s a theory of business cycles based upon sun spots affecting harvests – an idea of little moment except that it generated a search for a more satisfactory explanation. In subsequent decades cycles were linked with expansions and contractions in credit and later, in Keynesian analysis, with the multiplier and the accelerator processes.

Each business cycle is associated with a *boom* period in which consumer demand is rising quickly and investment and business profits are high. This is followed by a period of *recession* when the growth in consumer demand and profitability slows down and investment, production and employment are reduced. The third phase involves a period of trade *slump* in which there is heavy unemployment, unused industrial capacity, perhaps stable or falling prices and low business confidence. Eventually, however, the slump phase turns into a period of economic *recovery* as investment and employment pick up and business confidence returns. In turn, this leads to a new boom period and the cycle begins all over again. This pattern of economic activity is illustrated in Figure 4.9.

Keynes argued that the multiplier and accelerator effects combined explained the nature of business cycles. If firms face an increase in actual demand (or even expected demand) that cannot be met from existing

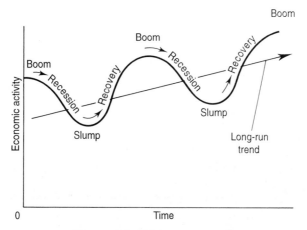

Figure 4.9 The business cycle.

capacity, they will invest in more capital equipment. Since additional investment expenditure (I) is an injection into the circular flow of income, the level of national income (Y) will rise and by more than the initial increase in investment because of the multiplier effect. The rise in national income itself may stimulate a further rise in consumption expenditure, which leads to more investment through the accelerator process, and so on. The interrelationship between the accelerator and the multiplier effects in business cycles can be summarized as follows:

$$\Delta I \rightarrow k \rightarrow \Delta Y \rightarrow a \rightarrow \Delta I \rightarrow k \rightarrow \Delta Y \ldots .$$

where a denotes the accelerator effect and k the multiplier effect. In relation to Figure 4.9 an initial rise in investment leads to higher incomes through the multiplier effect. The rise in income in turn leads to more consumer demand and, through the accelerator effect, a further increase in the pace of investment, and so on. This process occurs in the recovery and boom phases of the business cycle. Similarly, during the recession and slump stages a reduction in investment leads to a fall in incomes, less consumer demand, more cancelled investment programmes and so forth, with the multiplier and accelerator effects working in reverse. Together the multiplier and accelerator effects exaggerate the economic consequences of any initial small changes in demand.

Less obvious, perhaps, is why a boom, once it is underway, comes to an end or why, once an economy goes into a slump, the end result is not total economic collapse. The explanation lies in *turning points* in the business cycle. In a period of economic expansion economic bottlenecks eventually emerge, notably shortages of labour, raw materials and perhaps energy. In addition, high investment may increase the cost of credit (interest rates). The overall effect is to drive up the costs of firms' inputs. The rise in costs in turn pushes up output prices leading eventually to a fall in the rate of growth of demand for goods and services. Higher prices may also lead to government action to deflate demand through fiscal and monetary measures to prevent accelerating inflation. These deflationary pressures eventually affect demand in the economy, leading to a slowdown in investment.

A turning point also occurs when economies are in recession. Although businesses will initially cancel investments when trade slackens, it is very unlikely that investment will contract to zero. Some investment must occur if production is to continue at all over the longer term, if only to replace the existing stock of capital as it wears out (depreciates). Therefore, there will be a floor to the level of investment. In addition, after a period of economic contraction cost pressures, including interest rates and perhaps wage rates, tend to ease, leading to new business opportunities. Eventually the economic decline is reversed.

Concluding remarks

In this chapter we have considered both how an equilibrium level of national income is determined and the Keynesian notion of an equilibrium level of national income below or above the economy's full employment level. We looked, in particular, at the composition of aggregate demand and the effect of changes in aggregate demand on national income and therefore employment and inflation. Especially important is the process by which changes in aggregate demand affect the economy through the multiplier and accelerator effects. Together these effects provide key insights into the nature of the business cycle and fluctuations in economic activity.

In the next chapter we turn to the use of fiscal policy by governments to smooth out economic fluctuations arising from the business cycle. Can governments, by changing taxes and public spending, offset the effects on the level of economic activity of fluctuations in private sector consumption and investment expenditure so that the economy can be maintained at full employment with stable prices? In the post-war period, Keynesian economists thought they could. Today, however, many economists are sceptical on theoretical grounds and because of the experience of economic management in the post-war years. Indeed, some economists challenge the core feature of Keynesian economics – the notion of an equilibrium national income with unemployment (at least over the longer term) in market economies. They prefer to emphasize that in competitive, free market economies all goods and services should be sold and all labour employed through variations in wages and prices. Therefore, there is no need for state interference in the form of aggregate demand management using fiscal policy. Indeed, some argue that state interference is a principal *cause* of inflation and unemployment because it undermines the smooth operation of the market economy. These ideas are explored in Chapters 6 and 7.

5

Management of the economy I: Fiscal policy

The essence of fiscal policy

In Chapter 4 demand management was defined as government policy measures directed at attempting to influence the level of aggregate demand (*AD*) in the economy and hence the level of economic activity. In this chapter, we shall examine the importance of a particular type of policy in this context, namely *fiscal policy*. The idea of using fiscal policy for demand management stems largely from the work of the Cambridge economist John Maynard Keynes in the 1930s and is concerned with manipulating taxation (personal and/or corporate) and government expenditure to influence the level of economic activity. Remember that an increase in government expenditure (*G*) is referred to as an *injection* into the circular flow of income. Hence, an increase in G will expand aggregate demand and, if the economy has sufficient spare capacity to meet this extra demand, physical production (i.e. *real* national income) and employment will also increase. In contrast, taxation is referred to as a *leakage*, such that an increase in taxes will reduce aggregate demand and the level of economic activity (similarly, a cut in government expenditure or a reduction in taxation will have opposite effects on the economy to those just outlined).

In the previous chapter we also identified how inflationary and deflationary gaps between aggregate demand and full employment output with stable prices could arise. Keynes was particularly concerned with the deflationary gap when he wrote *The General Theory of Employment, Interest and Money* (1936). The 1930s were a time of high unemployment. In the post-war years, however, Keynesian economists were more concerned with keeping down inflation. Keynes had argued that government

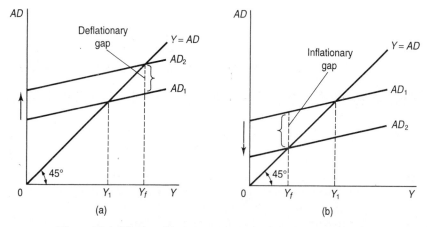

Figure 5.1 Closing (a) deflationary and (b) inflationary gaps.

spending and taxation levels could be used to eliminate a deflationary gap in the economy. The resulting rise in public or private spending could produce a sustained rise in economic activity. Keynesians argued that an inflationary gap could be removed in a similar way by provoking a fall in public or private spending.

To close a deflationary gap (where the equilibrium level of national income is below the full employment level) and thus increase aggregate demand so as to raise national income, the government could either raise government expenditure or reduce taxation levels. Either of these measures would produce a multiple rise in demand through the *multiplier* effect discussed in Chapter 4. In contrast, to close an inflationary gap (where the equilibrium level of national income exceeds the full employment level), the government could either reduce government expenditure or raise taxation levels. Again these measures, Keynesians argued, would have the effect of reducing aggregate demand, this time through a negative multiplier effect. Figure 5.1 illustrates both cases.

In Figure 5.1(a) fiscal measures cause aggregate demand to rise from AD_1 to AD_2 leading to an increase in national income from Y_1 to Y_f. In Figure 5.1(b) the level of aggregate demand is reduced from AD_1 to AD_2 leading to a decrease in national income from Y_1 to Y_f. In both cases Y_f represents an equilibrium level of national income with full employment and stable prices. Also, note that the change in aggregate demand in both figures is smaller than the resulting change in national income. The difference reflects the multiplier effect. Fiscal policy, used in this manner, is often described as a policy of *fine-tuning* aggregate demand to maintain equilibrium national income at full employment output without inflation. Referring back to our earlier discussion of business cycles (pages 70–2), the central message of Keynesian economics is that governments can smooth out cyclical fluctuations in national income. Therefore, as business cycles are endemic to free market economies, Keynesian economics identifies a continuing role for the state to monitor and influence the level of aggregate demand.

The use of fiscal policy measures by the government to influence intentionally the level of economic activity gives rise to the label *discretionary* fiscal policy. In contrast, there is a sense in which fiscal policy helps to stabilize economic activity automatically. For instance, if the level of unemployment rises, tax revenue to the government will tend to decline (income tax revenues will fall as incomes contract and less spending leads to lower VAT receipts), while government expenditure on the various forms of welfare benefits will rise, unless the government takes positive steps to stop this happening. The fall in tax revenue represents a reduction in a leakage from the circular flow of income, while the increase in government spending represents a larger injection into the circular flow. Combined, these effects result in aggregate demand falling less quickly than in the absence of government involvement in the economy. Fiscal policy in this context is referred to as an *automatic stabilizer*, i.e. there has been no deliberate action on the part of the government to alleviate any fall in aggregate demand due to rising unemployment, but it occurs automatically once the change in economic activity takes place.

Problems with fine-tuning aggregate demand

In the post-war period through to the mid-1970s a number of Western countries, especially the UK, attempted to fine-tune aggregate demand using fiscal policy (often coupled with some monetary measures such as changes in interest rates – see the discussion of monetary policy in the next chapter). Up to the late 1960s UK unemployment remained low in most years, which seems to suggest that the policy was successful. On the other hand, the reconstruction of the continental European economies after the war, with more international economic co-operation, for example with regard to exchange rates (see the discussion of exchange rates in Chapter 9), and increased free trade supervised by the General Agreement on Tariffs and Trade (GATT) signed in 1947, led to an unparalleled expansion in world trade from which the UK benefited. The extent, therefore, to which low unemployment was the product of Keynesian fine-tuning remains controversial. Certainly in the 1970s, both unemployment and inflation rose, leading to *stagflation*, which Keynesian economics appeared unable to tackle through fiscal measures alone. From a Keynesian viewpoint, to reverse rising unemployment requires reducing taxes and increasing government spending to boost aggregate demand. Higher inflation, in contrast, requires the opposite, that is higher taxation and reduced public spending to lower total demand in the economy. Clearly, both policies cannot be pursued at the same time.

One possible solution, much favoured by Keynesian economists in the 1960s and 1970s and pursued by governments at that time, was the introduction of a *prices and incomes policy*. The idea was that inflation could be confined by voluntary or mandatory limits on wage and price increases, while at the same time fiscal measures were used to support employment. The history of prices and incomes policies in the UK is not, however, a happy one. While they succeeded initially in restraining wage demands, they eventually broke down as workers refused to accept a reduction in real incomes. This breakdown led to a wage–price explosion, which occurred most dramatically in the coal miners' strike of 1974 and the 'winter of discontent' of 1978/9. The failure of prices and incomes policies to provide much more than a breathing space in the battle against inflation is not too surprising when we recall that they merely hold down cost increases coming from wages. They do nothing to tackle other sources of inflation, for example excess aggregate demand resulting from high public spending.

As a means of fine-tuning aggregate demand, government spending and taxation were limited in their effects for a number of reasons:

1. The full impact of government spending programmes (such as in the case of major capital projects) often took a long time to feed through into aggregate demand, reducing the ability of governments to fine-tune economic activity successfully.
2. Once state expenditure was increased it proved difficult to reverse the spending. It made no sense to the electorate to leave bridges, roads, hospitals, etc., half built, and once pensions and other welfare provisions were increased it was not politically easy to attempt to reduce them.
3. The cost of large-scale government projects had a tendency to escalate out of all proportion to original estimates once the projects had commenced (recall the experience with Concorde in the late 1960s and early 1970s and the Nimrod early warning radar project in the mid-1980s, which was eventually abandoned).
4. Taxation, including national insurance contributions, as a percentage of GDP drifted upwards in the early 1960s to the mid-1970s – on one measure from around 32 per cent to 45 per cent of GDP at market prices. In other words, governments raised taxes to finance higher public spending more often than they reduced them.

In general, government spending plans were politically sensitive and therefore could not be directed to fine-tune aggregate demand in the manner Keynesian economists recommended. (How many political parties before 1979 were elected on the basis of promising to *reduce* government expenditure, even if cuts were justified from a macroeconomic viewpoint?) From the 1960s some economists began to put forward an alternative view of government spending and taxation under the banner of *public choice theory*. Under the Keynesian approach, governments are expected to operate as objective or disinterested regulators of the economy, altering taxation and public spending in the public interest to smooth out the business cycle. But why should the politicians that direct policy and the civil servants who administer it be disinterested parties? Presumably politicians seek re-election and re-election is linked to winning public popularity by spending more, for instance, on schools and hospitals, rather than less. Similarly, civil servants are most likely to benefit directly in terms of status, promotion prospects, continued employment, size of budgets handled, and so forth, if public spending programmes grow, not if they are curtailed. Public choice theory therefore dismisses the notion of disinterested fine-tuning of demand and explains the raising of public spending and taxation in terms of politicians and government administrators pursuing their own interests rather than the public interest. This viewpoint appears to have been influential, alongside monetarism, in shaping the UK government's approach to state spending in the 1980s.

So far we have discussed the essence of fiscal policy from the viewpoint of its role as a demand management instrument. We turn now, however, to a more general analysis of government expenditure and taxation decisions in terms of the overall structure and significance of public sector finances and their impact upon business.

Public finance

There are three broad elements to public sector finance:

1. expenditures at national and local levels;
2. taxation to provide an income to government in order to finance these expenditure plans;
3. borrowing if expenditure exceeds income.

Expenditure

Governments spend vast sums of money on our behalf from one year to the next for a wide variety of purposes. This expenditure represents a major injection into the circular flow of income, and as such is an important source of increases in the level of national income. The injection takes place at three levels:

1. at the national level by the central government;
2. at the local level through local authorities;
3. through publicly-owned corporations.

All of this expenditure takes the form of both current account expenditure (such as books for schools, notepaper for government offices, etc.) and capital account expenditure (buildings, roads, etc.). In addition to current and capital account items, transfer payments are also made by central and local government, for example pensions, child and housing benefits. All of these categories of expenditure play a major role in the smooth running of an economy in terms of the provision of public and social services, job creation and redistribution of the national income across different sectors of society.

Table 5.1 provides details of UK public spending as a percentage of GDP since the early 1960s. It will be seen that the share of public spending in total domestic output rose from the early 1960s to the mid-1970s. It then fell following stringent cuts in public spending by the Labour government in 1975/6. It rose again from the late 1970s due to more spending on defence (intended) and social security at a time of high unemployment (unintended). As the economic recessions abated, the share of public spending in output fell slowly until it reached nearly 39 per cent by the fiscal year 1988/9. The recession of the early 1990s, however, led to a sharp reversal of the downward trend with public spending exceeding 44 per cent of GDP by 1992/3.

Government expenditure has important implications for the business community. Any element of government expenditure which is not spent on imported goods and services potentially raises the level of demand in the domestic economy for the goods and services produced by domestic firms. This is equally true whether the expenditure takes the form of transfer payments to the household sector, subsidies or grants to the business sector itself, or direct government spending. Through the multiplier effect (reinforced by the accelerator effect) the initial increase in government spending will lead to an even greater increase in the demand for the output of the business sector, boosting aggregate demand as a whole. Balanced against this, however, government spending has to be financed.

Taxation: sources and uses

Government income comes from a variety of sources, the main one being *taxation*. Other sources, which need only a brief mention here, are:

Table 5.1 Total UK public spending as a
percentage of GDP.[a]

	Total spending as a percentage of GDP
1963/4	36.8
1969/70	41.0
1974/5	48.8
1978/9	44.0
Conservative government	
1979/80	44.0
1980/1	46.5
1981/2	47.3
1982/3	47.5
1983/4	46.5
1984/5	46.8
1985/6	45.0
1986/7	44.0
1987/8	41.8
1988/9	39.3
1989/90	39.8
1990/1	40.3
1991/2	42.0
1992/3	44.5
1993/4	44.3
1994/5	42.8
1995/6[c]	42.0
1996[b]/7[c]	40.5

[a] Public spending is defined for the purpose of
   these figures as General Government Expenditure
   (excluding privatization receipts).
[b] Estimate.
[c] Forecast.
Source: HM Treasury, Autumn Financial Statement
(various issues); CSO, *Economic Trends*, annual
supplements

1. national insurance contributions;

2. surpluses of public corporations;

3. rent, interest and dividends earned by central and local government;

4. sales of public assets (i.e. privatization proceeds);

5. direct charges to users of government services (e.g. use of beds by
   private patients in public-sector hospitals, prescription charges for
   medicines etc.).

The primary function of taxation is to raise revenue to finance
government expenditure but it may also be used to influence expenditure

patterns (or the general level of aggregate demand as noted above), to redistribute income and wealth, and to reflect other social and political objectives. It is also tempting to look upon taxation as an 'evil' in that it can deter companies from investing more capital when high corporate tax reduces the potential returns. High personal taxation may also deter individuals from working harder to earn more, perhaps encouraging the 'black economy' in which people work for cash and do not declare their income for tax purposes. Evidence with regard to the extent that taxation *causes* a disincentive to either work or invest is, however, not conclusive (we return to this issue in Chapter 7 in discussing the role of tax cuts as a supply-side measure to stimulate output and employment).

The primary functions of taxation may be summarized as follows:

1. To raise sufficient revenue for both central and local government to finance expenditure.

2. To redistribute wealth from the better-off to the less well-off – in the UK, for example, via income tax, capital gains tax and inheritance tax and then via transfer payments to the less well-off in society.

3. Taxes, in the form of import tariffs and duties, may be used to protect domestic industries from foreign competition (see Chapter 8 for further details).

4. Taxes may also be levied on certain products to take account of their 'social costs'; for example, tax revenue from cigarette sales helps to offset the cost to the nation arising from health care for those suffering from smoking-related diseases, while the tax itself may be an incentive to give up smoking. Likewise, tax on petrol may help to encourage economy with regard to petrol consumption and hence reduce pollution from car emissions.

Political debates concerning taxation are more or less continuous nowadays, especially around budget time each year. These debates generally reflect differing views about what is or is not a 'good' tax system and structure. Clearly, it is not possible to provide a statement of absolute truth in this matter but we can identify some general principles. In general terms, a tax system may be deemed good if it is structured such that:

1. The amount of tax to be paid is easily understood by everyone.

2. Payment is convenient (e.g. via payrolls or via tax on expenditure, such as VAT on certain types of goods and services).

3. Collection costs are minimal compared with the amount of tax collected so that net revenues are maximized; similarly, compliance costs (cost .

individuals and businesses of complying with the payment of taxes, e.g. operating the VAT system) should be kept as low as possible.

4. Tax rates can readily be adjusted up or down to reflect changing economic (or political) circumstances.

5. Work, investment and enterprise are not discouraged because of high tax levels, otherwise economic activity and tax revenues will suffer through disincentive effects.

6. Avoidance of the tax is difficult.

These principles are generally agreed. Some economists argue, however, that a further requirement is that people should pay taxes according to their ability to pay. This is far more controversial because it may conflict with the goals of minimizing evasion and collection costs and may discourage work and enterprise. In addition, this issue has strong political undertones – consider, for example, the controversy surrounding the Community Charge (or Poll Tax) system introduced in Scotland in 1989 and in England and Wales in 1990. Critics of the tax, which was later abandoned, argued that it took insufficient account of ability to pay.

The various types of tax collected by the government may be categorized in a number of ways:

- progressive;
- regressive;
- proportional;
- direct;
- indirect.

Progressive taxes
A progressive tax is one which takes a greater proportion of people's income as their income rises. This is the type of income tax system used throughout Western economies. In the UK, for example, the percentage of tax paid on additional (marginal) income was either 25 or 40 per cent in 1994/5, depending on income level. The UK tax structure today, however, is much less progressive than it was in the past; in 1979 when the Conservative government was elected, the top rate on unearned income (interest, rent and dividends) was 98 pence in the pound and, on earned income (pensions, wages and salaries) 83 pence in the pound. According to critics of high taxation this led to a flood of tax exiles from the UK and encouraged tax avoidance (legal means to minimize taxes paid) and in some cases outright tax evasion (illegal tax dodging).

There are several arguments which can be made both for and against progressive tax systems. Generally, progressive taxes facilitate a redistribution of wealth from the rich to the poor and counterbalance, to some extent, the regressive nature of some other taxes which bear more heavily on the less well-off (see below). In addition, progressive taxation may be more politically acceptable to society insofar as it is regarded as socially just.

At the same time, however, high and progressive taxation can act as a deterrent to investment and initiative in both the business and household sectors, while encouraging tax evasion and the identification of loopholes within the system. It can also encourage a transfer of wealth to other countries or encourage the establishment of tax havens where tax rates are low. Moreover, progressive taxation may encourage growth in public spending, especially in democracies where the majority may vote for more spending on health, education, etc., while attempting to place the cost on the shoulders of a small, if richer, minority.

Regressive taxes
A regressive tax falls more lightly on high incomes rather than low incomes – that is, it takes proportionately more from those least able to pay. An example is the Community Charge which was introduced in England and Wales in April 1990 (and a year earlier in Scotland) as a means of financing local authority spending.

Proportional taxes
Proportional taxes take a set proportion or percentage of income. For example, UK income tax is broadly proportional, after the first £3,900 of taxable income, up to £25,500 in 1996/7 at a rate of 24 per cent ('broadly' because the existence of the lower rate tax at 20 per cent on the first £3,900 and personal allowances, which are deducted before taxable income is calculated, make the tax slightly progressive). Only above this income level does the UK income tax rate become more progressive when it rises to 40 per cent.

The difference between progressive, regressive and proportional income taxes is summarized in Figure 5.2.

Direct taxes
Direct taxes are those applied *directly* to the incomes of individuals and companies and to transfers of income and wealth. In the UK such taxes are paid to the Inland Revenue, the main categories being income tax, corporation tax, capital gains tax, inheritance tax, petroleum revenue tax on North Sea production and stamp duty (in addition, national insurance

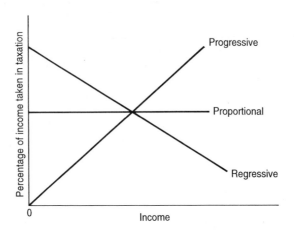

Figure 5.2 Contrasting progressive, regressive and proportional income taxes.

contributions for employees, though not strictly a tax, are mainly collected via the income tax PAYE system by the Inland Revenue and paid over to the Departments of Health and Social Security). Direct taxes tend to be progressive or proportional. Their main advantages, at least from the government's viewpoint, are the generally low collection costs and the fact that payment of them is usually difficult to avoid. For example, the cost of collecting income tax is usually around 2 per cent of revenue in the UK, due largely to the efficient PAYE system, while recent estimates put the size of the black economy in the UK at around 7 per cent of GDP (compared with some estimates of over 20 per cent in Italy). Much of the tax evasion occurs in the self-employed sector of the economy where PAYE does not operate.

Indirect taxes
Indirect taxes, which tend to be regressive in nature, are applied to expenditure and the value added to production. The main indirect tax in Europe is VAT, collected from an intermediary (for example, a shopkeeper) who then passes the tax on to the consumer in the price of goods sold. Other indirect taxes are excise duties on spirits and beers and customs duties on imported goods.

Advantages and disadvantages of direct taxation
Direct taxes are potentially 'fair' or equitable in that they can be levied according to ability to pay (if governments choose to do so). They also act, to some degree, as automatic stabilizers (see page 76) in that the amount of

tax revenue rises sharply when national income is rising, thereby increasing the leakage effect from the circular flow of income and taking some inflationary 'heat' out of the economy. Direct taxes are also less inflationary than indirect taxes since they are not levied on expenditure and therefore do not raise the price of goods and services directly.

Two disadvantages of the main direct tax, namely income tax, are often stressed: these refer to the possibility of a *poverty trap* and a *fiscal drag effect*. The combination of income tax, national insurance contributions and the possible loss of earnings-related welfare benefits as income rises, can result in an extra £1 of earned income leading to a decrease in an individual's disposable income. This represents an effective tax rate on additional income (known as the marginal rate of tax) of over 100 per cent on some low-income earners. This situation is known as the *poverty trap* and is clearly a disincentive to working. It undoubtedly also encourages activity in the black economy. In recent years, however, the raising of personal tax allowances (i.e. thresholds at which taxation begins), changes in the rates of national insurance contributions on low incomes, and reform of welfare benefits seem to have reduced the incidence of the poverty trap in the UK.

An additional problem with direct income tax arises when personal allowances and tax thresholds (at which higher marginal rates come into effect) are not increased in line with the general rate of price inflation. In this situation, income tax payments will tend to rise in real terms as people are 'dragged' into higher tax brackets or become liable to pay tax for the first time – this process is referred to as *fiscal drag* and could lead to higher wage demands as workers attempt to compensate for earnings lost in tax. In the 1980s, with the exception of one year, 1981/2, the UK government increased personal allowances and tax thresholds by at least the rate of inflation to offset fiscal drag. In the early 1990s, however, a number of allowances were frozen by the government, thereby reducing their real value and creating a significant fiscal drag effect. This was done to raise tax revenue in an effort to reduce an historically high PSBR (see page 87).

Advantages and disadvantages of indirect taxation

It is argued that indirect taxes are preferable to direct taxes in that the consumer has the choice of not paying the tax (e.g. VAT) by simply not consuming the taxed good. Indirect taxes can also be levied on particular types of goods at different rates in order to encourage or discourage consumption (e.g. cigarettes). In this way, the allocation of the nation's resources may be changed from production of certain goods to other, more 'desirable' goods. On the other hand, indirect taxes may conceal the true tax burden that people face because they are hidden: the consumer may be unaware of the precise amount of tax that he or she is paying.

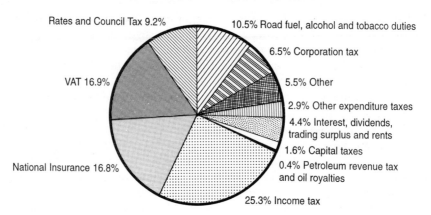

Figure 5.3 Sources of UK tax revenue 1993/4. *Source*: From data in HM Treasury, *Financial Statement and Budget Report*, HMSO, London, p. 76.

Indirect taxation is a flexible policy weapon insofar as the rates may be altered quickly and easily with immediate effect. This is useful from the government's standpoint in terms of the speed with which aggregate demand may be stimulated. At the same time, however, indirect taxes such as VAT tend to have an inflationary impact on the economy. By raising retail prices by the amount of the tax levied, there is a danger that this will tend to push up wage demands and may lead to a wage–price–wage spiral. Also, as noted above, indirect taxes tend to be regressive in nature, though a system of indirect taxes on luxury goods would be less regressive than, say, taxes on goods accepted as 'essentials' (e.g. televisions, furniture, etc.). A summary of the sources of UK tax revenue for 1993/4 is shown in Figure 5.3.

As noted earlier, government expenditure is financed largely by tax revenue. However, when total expenditure exceeds this revenue, the government, just like any firm or household, has to borrow to finance the difference. We now turn to this aspect of public sector finance which has a major role to play in the operation of fiscal policy as a demand management instrument.

Government borrowing

Deficit financing

The annual budget speech is the occasion when the government's expenditure and revenue plans for the coming year are confirmed. The budget represents the government's fiscal strategy or fiscal stance. For example, the *fiscal stance* at a time of a deflationary gap may be one of *deficit financing* whereby the government seeks to boost the economy by planning for a budget deficit (i.e. government expenditure is planned to exceed tax revenue). The effect of this is intended to be an expansion of aggregate demand leading to more income and employment through the multiplier effect. On the other hand, if the economy is overheating (i.e. an inflationary gap is emerging), the government could budget for a surplus of revenues over government spending in order to slow down the general level of economic activity. In this way, the budget is a major policy instrument available to a government to help it achieve particular economic objectives, for example higher employment, faster economic growth and lower inflation.

The public sector borrowing requirement (PSBR)

In the UK the amount of money which the public sector borrows during a given financial year is called the *public sector borrowing requirement* (PSBR). The size of the PSBR is broadly determined by a number of factors, namely:

1. the size of the budget deficit of central and local government;
2. the size of the deficit of nationalized industries and other public corporations financed by borrowing from non-government sources;
3. the public sector's receipts from the sale of real assets (e.g. the proceeds from privatization).

When there is a negative PSBR (that is when total tax revenues exceed total public sector expenditure) there is a budget surplus which is referred to in the UK as the *public sector debt repayment* (or PSDR). A PSDR means that the government is in a position to repay some of its accumulated borrowings from previous years which make up the *national debt*.

A balanced budget

When the totals of government spending (G) and taxation (T) are the same in any year, this situation is referred to as a *balanced budget*. It is important to appreciate, however, that a balanced budget is not the same as a *neutral* budget. A budget stance is said to be neutral when the level of aggregate demand in the economy and hence economic activity is left unaltered. In contrast, comparable expenditure and tax changes within the context of a balanced budget will not have the same effects upon aggregate demand and on national income. Consider the following example.

Suppose that the government raises its expenditure (G) by £1bn, financed entirely by an increase in tax revenue (T) of £1bn leaving the overall budget balanced. Assume also that consumers spend 80 per cent of any increase in their incomes while 20 per cent is saved. That is, the marginal propensity to consume (*mpc*) = 0.8 and the marginal propensity to save (*mps*) = 0.2. Ignoring the effect of taxation, the initial injection due to an increase in G will boost aggregate demand and will eventually result in national income (Y) rising by:

$$\Delta Y = \frac{1}{mps} \Delta G = 5 \times £1bn = £5bn$$

This is as a consequence of the multiplier effect (see Chapter 4 for an explanation of the *mpc*, the *mps* and the multiplier).

At the same time, however, the increase in taxation will have caused a rise in leakages from the circular flow of income which act to reduce the effect of injections of extra demand on the level of national income. Taking account of taxation makes the net result of the rise in government spending and taxation less straightforward than our example suggests. Part of any increase in taxation may be financed by reducing the rate of *savings*. To the extent that this happens, then the increase of the leakage due to taxation will be offset by a reduction in a second leakage, savings. In other words, the *net* change in leakages is less than the change in taxation. Consequently, only that part of any increase in taxation which is financed by a reduction in consumer spending will affect the level of aggregate demand and national income. The initial impact of this will be given by 0.8 × ΔT (i.e. *mpc* × the change in taxation) which will have a (negative) multiplier effect on aggregate demand in general, equal to:

$$\frac{mpc \times \Delta T}{mps} = \frac{0.8(£1bn)}{0.2} = £4bn$$

Hence, the *net* result of an equivalent increase in G and T is that national income rises by (£5bn − £4bn) = £1bn. The *balanced budget multiplier* in this situation is therefore equal to 1 (i.e. ΔY/ΔG = £1bn).

In general, allowing for savings, taxation and also imports, a balanced budget will have an expansionary effect on national income, as in our example. The impact of expenditure upon imports is reflected in the balanced budget multiplier in exactly the same way as savings.

Criticisms of fiscal policy and deficit financing

Traditional Keynesian demand management techniques place considerable emphasis on the use of the budget to influence the level of economic activity, as discussed earlier in this chapter and in the last chapter. It was conventional for governments in the post-war years to run a budget deficit financed by borrowing. From the early 1950s UK governments ran budget deficits in all but one financial year (1969/70) until 1986. After 1986 the government had sizeable budget surpluses until the recession of the early 1990s. The UK government's budgetary stance since the 1980s is set out in Figure 5.4.

During the 1970s, however, concern began to grow among economists about the economic effects of persistent deficit financing. This was especially true among *monetarists* (see Chapter 6). While these economists recognized the importance of fiscal policy from a budgetary viewpoint, they had a number of criticisms to make about the way in which fiscal policy measures, via the budget, were directed at controlling aggregate demand in the economy. Essentially, monetarists expressed concern regarding the effect that government deficit financing (i.e. a PSBR) had on the money supply and hence inflation. They dismissed direct management

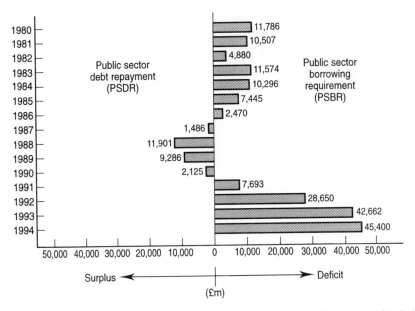

Figure 5.4 UK budgetary stance: 1980–94. *Sources*: *Annual Abstract of Statistics*, London, HMSO; *United Kingdom National Accounts*, London, HMSO, 1994 edition (note: dates are to 31 March in year shown).

of aggregate demand and national income via fiscal policy as potentially destabilizing and indeed argued that this sort of policy had little impact upon the 'real' economy in the long run. By the real economy they were referring to the growth in physical output, and therefore employment, as against a rise in prices which leads to a growth only in the money value of production.

In more specific terms, the monetarist criticisms of fiscal policy and deficit financing may be summarized under the following headings.

Intervention versus the free market

Keynesians and monetarists tend to disagree about the role of the state in managing the economy. On the one hand, monetarists tend to favour free enterprise and competition, arguing that government intervention via demand management and fiscal policy measures hampers competitive forces and discourages an enterprise culture. They also maintain that government expenditure is used as a prop for declining industries and hence fosters and perpetuates inefficient production. At the same time, high taxation to finance this expenditure, they argue, impedes the development of new growth industries. This critical view of the role of government and the use of fiscal policy can be readily associated with the approach of Mrs Thatcher's administration in the 1980s to state intervention in the economy.

Destabilizing the economy

Keynesian economists regard fiscal policy as an effective way to dampen down the economic fluctuations associated with the business cycle. Monetarists, however, argue that, far from dampening these fluctuations, fiscal policy has had the effect of destabilizing the economy by exaggerating the booms and slumps. They argue that this has largely been due to attempts by successive governments in the past to maintain aggregate demand at unsustainable high levels. This has thereby built up inflationary pressures, which have been further fed by more government spending and by the printing of 'excess' money (see Chapter 6) to ward off rising unemployment as industry became less competitive.

Impact of deficit financing on private sector investment

Monetarists also argue that if the government borrows to finance budget deficits, this forces up rates of interest in the financial markets. While the government has the ability to pay increased interest charges, either by raising taxes or by borrowing even more funds, the same does not apply to private sector firms. Faced with higher interest rates, they may be forced to cut back on investment plans. In addition, as interest rates rise, the exchange rate is also likely to be pushed up (see Chapter 9 for a discussion of the relationship between interest rates and exchange rates). A rise in the external value of the currency will damage firms' competitive position leading to a reduction in exports – while this in turn may cause still further cut-backs in investment expenditure as well as in employment.

This phenomenon, whereby increased government expenditure financed by increased borrowing may lead to a reduction in private sector investment, is referred to by economists as *crowding out* (i.e. government borrowing crowds out private sector borrowing in the capital markets). It must be said that in the case of the UK, evidence regarding the existence of crowding out is not conclusive. Studies undertaken in the USA, however, do point to some support for this criticism of government borrowing. As world capital markets become more and more integrated and as the growth of multinational companies which can tap various capital markets continues, the relevance of crowding out is likely to diminish. It is unlikely that one government's borrowing, even when large, will have a significant impact upon the availability of worldwide capital funds for private investment.

Impact upon money supply growth

Monetarists argue that a persistent PSBR forces the government into greater borrowing from the banking sector, causing the money supply to grow much faster than the output of goods and services, leading to inflation (the process by which this takes place will be discussed in the next chapter). A common monetarist slogan to sum this up is: 'too much money chasing too few goods causes inflation'. As the money supply and inflation grow, the international competitiveness of firms declines and unemployment rises.

Monetarists, therefore, preach that governments should not try to manage aggregate demand directly but, instead, should focus their efforts on trying to create a stable economic environment in which private enterprise can flourish. They argue that this is most readily achieved by reducing state intervention, balancing the government budget from year to year, and controlling the amount of money circulating in the economy in order to diminish inflationary pressures and expectations of inflation.

Concluding remarks

In this chapter we have studied the nature of fiscal policy, trends in fiscal policy in recent years and its use as a countercyclical tool. The notion that government, by changing the levels of taxation and public expenditure, can significantly influence aggregate demand and hence the level of economic activity proved attractive in the post-war period. Up to the mid-1970s, governments in the UK pursued policies which were largely Keynesian. However, the onset of stagflation (i.e. rising inflation and rising unemployment) coupled with the failure of prices and incomes policies led to a policy reappraisal. First, research identified failures in operating countercyclical (i.e. stop–go) policies – in particular there seemed to be a built in 'ratchet effect' in which government spending and taxation rose but were rarely cut back, leading to what appeared to critics to be an ever-expanding state sector. Second, the theory that lay behind Keynesian economics, and which justified demand management by fiscal policy, was challenged by the rise of an alternative school of thought in economics, monetarism, which we now detail.

6

Management of the economy II: Monetary policy

The essence of monetary policy

Monetary policy is generally concerned with any measures used by the government to influence the availability or price of money (i.e. the rate of interest) in an economy. In the UK, the responsibility for operating the government's monetary policy rests, through Her Majesty's Treasury, with the Bank of England. Growth in the importance of monetary policy as an instrument of macroeconomic management in recent years is explained to a large extent by the apparent failure of fiscal policy measures in the early 1970s to reduce the twin problems of inflation and unemployment – referred to as *stagflation*. As noted in the previous chapter, this failure was explained by monetarist economists in terms of excessive government spending financed by spiralling budget deficits. These deficits were financed not only through borrowing, from both the banking and non-banking sectors, but increasingly through the printing of new money. Both of these led to an increase in the money supply in excess of the amount needed to finance transactions arising from a growth in the physical output of the economy.

Monetarists argue that if the money supply is allowed to grow faster than the economy's output then households and firms will find themselves holding larger money balances than they desire to hold. This surplus of money balances will, therefore, be spent on goods and services leading to an increase in aggregate demand beyond the ability of the economy to supply. According to monetarists, this will result in a general rise in prices – an inflationary gap caused by excessive monetary growth. In addition, any upward pressure on prices will also fuel expectations of future inflation, resulting in higher wage demands and an ensuing danger of a wage–price–wage inflationary spiral. A related consequence of excessive monetary growth will then be rising unemployment as the competitiveness of firms declines and as workers price themselves out of jobs.

In the eyes of monetarists, unemployment can be brought down in the longer term only if the productive efficiency of the economy is increased and if inflationary expectations are diminished. It should be appreciated, however, that these monetarist views are not universally accepted by economists and governments. In particular, some economists (notably Keynesian economists) do not believe that controlling the growth in the money supply is necessarily the best way of bringing down inflation. Nor do they accept (as we have already seen in Chapter 5) that the only solution to unemployment is to reduce inflationary expectations and improve economic efficiency. This difference in policy prescriptions led in the 1960s and 1970s to a sharp division between economists into two schools of thought: Keynesians and monetarists. However, this distinction should not be exaggerated. Today many economists do not fit neatly into either camp, preferring to argue instead for a balance of policy measures, both monetary and fiscal, to influence economic activity.

In this chapter we set out more formally the principles of monetarism and the implications for aggregate demand and for government economic policy. We also discuss the main practical problems that have arisen in the implementation of monetary policy measures in the UK, as well as some of the criticisms levied at monetarism. Lastly, the effects of monetary policy measures on business, particularly with regard to the effect of interest rates upon the country's exchange rate, are also examined.

Principles of monetarism

At the most general level, it is not difficult to identify why money is important in the determination of aggregate demand. If the money supply is allowed to rise it will eventually mean that, first, people and firms have more money in their pockets or bank accounts and, second, interest rates in general will tend to fall. Consequently, consumers and investors will have the potential to affect aggregate demand through their purchasing power, that is they can use these funds to buy goods and services and for investment purposes such as purchasing government bonds and stocks and shares as well as investing in land and buildings. Increased consumer and investment spending then feed through into higher demand in the economy, affecting production, employment and inflation. This process by which a rise in the money supply affects aggregate demand and in turn money GDP (i.e. GDP at current prices) – what monetarists call the *money transmission mechanism* – is summarized in Figure 6.1. A rise in aggregate

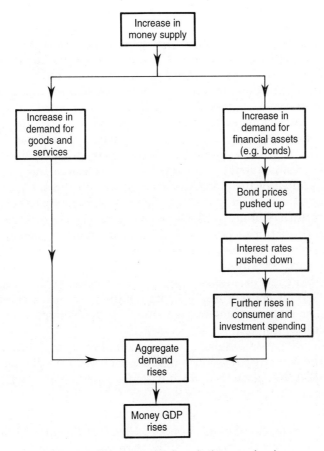

Figure 6.1 The money transmission mechanism.

demand may also have implications for the balance of payments if more imports are purchased (a discussion of this aspect of monetary growth is left until Chapter 9).

The significance of the role of money in the economy and the principles of monetarism are based on the *quantity theory of money,* which relates monetary growth to the rate of inflation. This relationship was first presented in formal terms by the American economist Irving Fisher in 1911, but the general idea that there is a link between a growth in the money supply and price rises dates back to the eighteenth century and particularly the writings of the Scottish philosopher David Hume. The quantity theory of money can be expressed in the following form:

$$MV = PT$$

where M is the supply of money in the economy, V the velocity of circulation of money around the economy, P the average price of all transactions in the economy, and T the total number of transactions in the economy in a particular time period. (Note that we previously used M to denote imports. It is, however, standard to denote the money supply by M also, and the context will clarify the meaning where necessary.)

The quantity theory is usually referred to as an identity rather than an equation because both sides of the expression are nothing more than equivalent ways of measuring economic activity: PT is a measure of the total expenditure in the economy, while MV is the total amount of money spent; both must be identical in money value. To clarify this even further, MV is the product of the amount of money available in the economy and the average number of times that this quantity of money passes around the economy as it is spent on transactions in a given time period, while PT is the value of those transactions. The stated equality must, by definition, be true although it should be appreciated that there are many measurement problems associated with its verification. For example, do we include in M only notes and coins or all forms of potential purchasing power, and how do we go about measuring the total number of transactions in the economy? The measurement of V is particularly problematic, despite much research on the subject.

Monetarists have traditionally made a number of assumptions which transform the $MV = PT$ relationship into a vehicle for predicting the likely impact of monetary growth upon inflation. In particular, they make two key assumptions:

1. The velocity of circulation of money (V) is believed to change very slowly over time and independently of changes in the money supply – therefore, it can be treated as a constant.

2. Since monetarists tend to believe that the economy has an in-built tendency to establish an equilibrium national income at full employment, it is assumed that the total number of transactions (T) is relatively constant in the short run (in other words, that T is restricted by the productive capacity of the economy at full employment).

These two assumptions relating to the constancy of V and T have been subject to much debate and criticism by economists over the years. We return to this issue later in the chapter, but for our present purposes we need only note from these monetarist principles that if V and T are constant then prices will vary directly with the amount of money in circulation. Moreover, on the basis of empirical testing, monetarists also argue that the direction of causation is from changes in M to changes in P and conclude that 'too much money chasing too few goods causes inflation'. In other words, and in very simplistic terms, if the money supply increases by 20 per cent then this should *eventually* lead to a 20 per cent increase in prices (in practice, the relationship is not so precise because V and T do not remain constant). The time taken for an increase in M to cause a rise in P is usually estimated to be around eighteen months to two years.

In addition to the above assumptions which are necessary to create a direct link between changes in the money supply and changes in prices, there are three further propositions to which all monetarists seem to subscribe. These are:

1. The money supply can be controlled by the authorities – this is necessary if governments are to target and control the rate of growth in the money supply to limit the growth of money GDP.

2. A competitive private sector economy automatically tends towards full employment. Therefore, there will be no long-term unemployment as envisaged by Keynes unless competition in markets (including the labour market) is impeded. For this reason monetarists reject Keynesian demand management policies, believing that they create uncertainty (with regard to investment, for example), and instead tend to favour supply-side reforms (see Chapter 7) alongside sound money policies.

3. By a sound money policy monetarists mean that there should be a steady rate of growth in the money supply, corresponding to the growth in real output, in order to achieve a stable level of prices. This gives rise to 'monetary targets', discussed below.

The validity of monetarist principles, like most theories in economics, is fundamentally dependent on the underlying assumptions being shown to be correct over time, in particular the constancy of V and T. However, quite apart from this, the testing of monetarism is also fraught with practical problems, not least with regard to measuring the quantity of money in circulation.

Measuring the money supply

What is money?

In principle, anything can be classified as money. The only condition is that whatever we decide to call money must be readily accepted as a medium of exchange (that is, individuals and firms must readily accept it in return for goods and services). For example, for a short time in Germany in 1945 cigarettes were traded for goods and services, hence they acted as a crude form of money. But normally, of course, we associate money with the notes and coins in our pockets issued by governments. These pieces of paper and metal carry the authority of government and are therefore usually readily accepted by individuals and businesses as a means of payment in day-to-day transactions. This does not always hold true, however, for confidence in a government's currency may cease to exist, for example in countries where there is very high inflation or political instability.

In addition to legally issued notes and coins we could include in a definition of money other forms of purchasing power, notably deposits held in bank current accounts and building society accounts which can be accessed easily. Like notes and coins, these are *liquid assets* because they can be quickly converted into cash at little if any loss. Why include only current accounts? Money can often be withdrawn fairly quickly from savings accounts, National Savings Certificates can be redeemed and securities such as government bills and bonds can be readily sold in the stock market. These are assets which are less liquid than cash and bank current accounts but can be quickly converted into cash, usually without a major financial penalty; they are therefore sometimes referred to as *quasi-money* or *near money*. Also, a good deal of consumer expenditure today is financed by credit, i.e. hire purchase finance, credit cards, etc. It should be appreciated, therefore, that there are problems in drawing a clear line between money and quasi-money and sometimes changes in the financial system invalidate previous distinctions. For example, in the UK since the mid-1980s, building societies have become more like banks, offering accounts almost identical to bank current accounts with cheque book facilities. For this reason building society deposits were included in one of the UK's official measures of money from the middle of 1987. Later, in 1989, the Bank of England stopped reporting definitions of the money supply which distinguished the deposits of building societies and banks.

A convenient way of illustrating the range of various measures of money is to think of a *liquidity spectrum*. Imagine that an individual's total assets can be classified along a scale of liquidity ranging from the most liquid to the least liquid. Obviously the most liquid asset will be cash, while the least liquid asset might be a person's house – especially if the owner cannot sell the house quickly, raise equity against it easily, or does not wish to sell it at all. Other assets can be placed between these two extremes accordingly. For example, bank current accounts will fall close to the liquid end of the spectrum, while a five-year fixed-term investment would lie towards the illiquid end, as illustrated in Figure 6.2. The idea of this personalized liquidity spectrum can be readily extended to the economy as a whole. For official purposes, however, governments do not measure monetary aggregates across the full range of the spectrum. Instead, in the UK, for

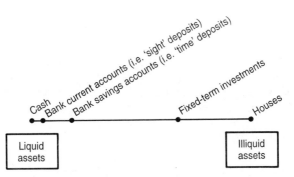

Figure 6.2 The liquidity spectrum.

example, the government focuses upon a limited range of assets, giving rise to various money supply measures (discussed below). Before turning to them it is important to understand the role of banks in the creation of money and the relationship between government borrowing (referred to in Chapter 5 as the PSBR) and the money supply.

Banks and the creation of money

Governments have the ability to increase the money supply by simply instructing their central bank (in the UK, the Bank of England) to print more bank notes. High Street banks (commercial banks) also have the ability to create money, however, even though in the UK they do not have the authority to produce their own currency. They can do this by the creation of bank deposits. Note that it is the bank deposits which create money, not cheques as such: cheques are merely the means of transferring bank deposits from one person to another. It is the bank deposit and not merely the cheque which is accepted in payment for goods and services. In the UK, commercial bank deposits are by far the most important component of the money supply, accounting for over 90 per cent of the value of all transactions.

There are three ways in which new bank deposits may be created:

1. When a bank receives a cash deposit from a customer.
2. When a bank makes a loan to a customer and this loan is then credited to the customer's current account with the bank.
3. When a bank purchases a security such as a bond leading to the deposit of the purchase price by the seller back into the banking system.

We can illustrate the impact of the first two cases upon the ability of banks to create credit and new deposits, and consequently, how these affect the money supply by the following simplified example. Imagine that a bank receives a cash deposit of £1,000 and the bank wishes to maintain a ratio of 10 per cent cash-to-total deposits (either for reasons of prudence or because it is required to do so by the authorities). It then has £900 available for lending to willing borrowers. If the bank lends up to this total in the form of advances, crediting these to customers' accounts, then its balance sheet will be affected as follows:

Liabilities	£	*Assets*	£
Deposit (initial)	1,000	Cash reserve	1,000
Deposit (new)	900	Advances	900
	1,900		1,900

Now suppose that the borrowers spend all of these advances (£900) with cash being drawn from the bank to meet these expenditures. Eventually this £900 will flow back to the bank as deposits from shopkeepers, etc. Now 90 per cent of these new deposits (£810) can be re-lent by the bank, assuming a continued cash-to-deposit ratio of 10 per cent (even where there are a number of banks rather than just a single bank, provided that they are increasing their advances at the same rate, they should receive new deposits at their branches of roughly the same amount as they lend out – therefore, the process by which deposits are created remains similar to the one in our example). Once more, these new advances (£810) will be spent and again will be redeposited. This process will continue until new deposits are negligible. It is apparent, therefore, from this simple explanation, that an initial increase in bank deposits of £1,000 cash leads to a multiple expansion of bank deposits related to the percentage cash reserve. In general, the eventual increase in deposits following an initial deposit of cash is given by:

Increase in deposits = Initial deposit × 1/cash-deposit ratio

The fraction, 1/cash-deposit ratio, is referred to as the *bank credit multiplier* (note that this is quite distinct from the national income multiplier discussed in Chapter 4). In our example, the initial deposit of £1,000 will lead to a £10,000 increase in total deposits (£1,000 × 1/0.1). It is obvious, therefore, that the extent to which the bank is able to create credit and hence its impact upon the money supply is dependent upon the cash-deposit ratio. In practice, banks may hold their assets in forms other than cash and advances, such as overnight lending to the money market and purchases of government Treasury bills (known as liquid assets because of their short-term nature) and government long-dated securities and equities (more illiquid asset forms). The holding of such assets will restrict the ability of banks to lend in the form of advances. Also, from time to time governments impose minimum requirements on banks with regard to these asset holdings in order to constrain credit expansion and hence the growth in the money supply. In the past few years, however, in the UK such restrictions have been almost entirely removed as part of a policy of deregulation in the financial sector.

Turning to the impact upon the money supply of a bank purchasing a security, there are two broad possibilities to consider. If the security is sold by the private sector and the money received is redeposited in the banking system, then we face the same situation as described above giving rise to a bank credit multiplier effect. On the other hand, if the security is sold by the government then the outcome is not so clear cut. The government can either spend the money which has been raised in this way (in which case the money will eventually find its way back into the banking system leading to a multiple expansion of credit as before) or it can retain the money as reserves. In the latter case this will result in a contraction in the bank's ability to lend and ultimately a contraction in total bank deposits and therefore the money supply. The purchase and sale of government securities in this manner to affect bank lending is referred to as *open market operations*. Indeed, the government can exercise its influence on the ability of banks to expand their lending by dealing across a wide spectrum of government securities with various dates to maturity, ranging from short-dated securities (90-day Treasury bills) to medium- and long-term government bonds. By replacing short-term government debt with longer-dated securities (a procedure known as *funding*) the authorities are able to reduce liquidity in the financial system including the banks.

Further methods by which a central bank can restrict credit creation by commercial banks involve special deposits and requests and directives. Special deposits were introduced in the UK in 1958 and involve the banks depositing cash at the Bank of England on which they earn interest at the Treasury bill rate but which they are unable to draw upon. These deposits are therefore illiquid assets and directly reduce the amount that the banks have available to lend. The Bank of England also has wide statutory powers to direct the activities of the banks. On occasions in the 1960s and 1970s, the Bank 'requested' or directed the banks to restrict their lending or to give priority to certain types of loan, for example loans associated with exporting. The government, through the Bank, also restricted bank credit by laying down maximum repayment periods, notably for car loans. Since 1980, the UK government has distanced itself from this type of direct intervention in bank credit creation for reasons discussed later.

Government borrowing and the money supply

A government can finance any excess of public expenditure over tax receipts simply by printing more money. In the UK, since the Bank of England is not a government department (technically it is a public corporation like the Post Office), this would involve the Treasury borrowing from the Bank of England against the issue of new government securities (referred to as gilt-edged securities). This would amount to the printing of new money because the Treasury and the Bank of England would merely swap one 'IOU' (gilt-edged securities) for another (bank notes). The result would be a direct increase in the money supply which feeds into the economy as government departments spend. As there would be no extra production associated with this monetary expansion, it would potentially be highly inflationary. Hence, in practice, most governments eschew this method of financing their deficits and borrow from sources other than the central bank. There are a number of ways in which governments can borrow:

1. By issuing non-marketable debt (National Savings) which is purchased by the non-bank private sector.

2. By issuing both short- and long-term marketable debt (Treasury bills and gilt-edged securities respectively). While the former is bought mainly by banks, the latter is also bought by the non-bank private sector or the overseas sector.

3. By borrowing from abroad.

The first two methods are usually the most important determinants of monetary growth. An increasing PSBR will have an effect on bank deposits because the lenders to the government will use money in their bank accounts to pay for the debt securities that they purchase. It is important to distinguish the effects of public sector borrowing from both the non-bank private sector and the banking system.

If the government borrows from the non-bank private sector – i.e. the public (individuals and firms) – by issuing new securities or by means of National Savings schemes, the initial effect will be a transfer of money from the commercial banks' deposits to the government, assuming that the securities are purchased by customers using cheques drawn on their bank accounts. In the first instance, the effect of this will be to reduce the amount of money in circulation. However, the government is borrowing to spend and the money raised will eventually be paid back in one form or another to the non-bank private sector. A proportion of this money will end up as notes and coins in people's pockets, but the bulk of it will return to the banking system in the form of bank deposits by customers.

Consequently, the money supply will be restored to an amount close to its original total. Therefore, in summary, when the government borrows money from the non-bank private sector there will be little net effect on the money supply, assuming that the government spends the money that it borrows, which will usually be the case. If the government did not spend the money borrowed, deposits at banks would, of course, fall leading to a contraction of the money supply. When the government borrows more than it needs to finance its spending this is known as a policy of *overfunding*. Overfunding was most recently practised in the UK in the mid-1980s as the government attempted to neutralize some of the growth in the money supply taking place at that time.

On the other hand, the government may decide to borrow from the banking system. When the banks purchase government securities, as we noted above, their cash base will be reduced. Assuming once again that the money received by the government is spent, this in turn will result in a transfer of cash from the government back to individuals and firms. If this cash is then deposited in the banking system we will again perceive an increase in the total volume of deposits. In essence, the total of bank deposits will have risen and there will initially be a direct increase in the money supply equal to the amount borrowed by the government from the banking system. This initial increase will then lead to a multiple expansion of bank deposits and hence a much greater increase in the money supply via the bank credit multiplier.

In conclusion, if the government wants to control monetary growth but is unable to reduce its PSBR, it should sell debt to the non-bank private sector. Borrowing from this source does not lead to an increase in the money supply. It should be appreciated, however, that this will have implications for the level of interest rates in the economy. The government will ultimately be competing for private sector savings with banks, building societies and other financial institutions, which will tend to drive up interest rates. When the government is prepared to accept lower prices for its securities in order to raise sufficient finance in competition with the financial institutions, this will raise the rate of return on these securities. This in turn leads to higher interest rates in the economy in general: i.e. there is an inverse relationship between the price of government securities and interest rates. As interest rates are driven up, particularly if the government needs to finance an ever-increasing PSBR, there is the danger, as noted in Chapter 5, of private sector investment being squeezed: the 'crowding out' effect.

It should be noted that reference to the money supply has so far assumed that it is defined narrowly in terms of cash and bank deposits. As we have already commented, though, money can take many forms so long as it is a readily accepted medium of exchange. We now consider official definitions in the UK.

Official definitions of the money supply in the UK

The various official definitions of the money supply in the UK are summarized in Figure 6.3. These monetary aggregates are distinguished as M0, M1, M2, M3 and M4, with extra forms of 'money' added as we progress through the series. For example, M4 is a much wider definition of the money supply than M1. The two monetary aggregates most often cited in the UK are M0 and M4, though the government put more store on M1 than M0 in 1982 and 1983, and on M3 than M4 throughout most of the 1980s until changes in the financial markets made the M3 measure redundant. M0 is the narrowest definition of money (sometimes referred to

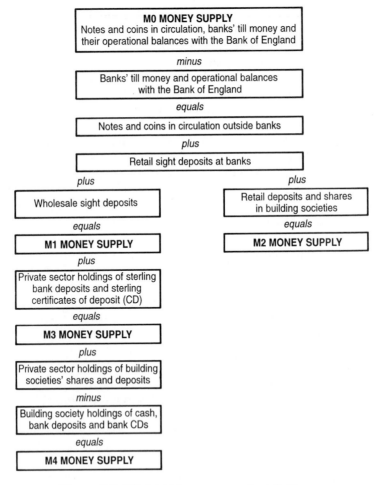

Figure 6.3 Official UK money supply definitions.

as *narrow money* or the *monetary base*) and includes only notes and coins in circulation, the money that commercial banks hold in their tills and their operational balances held at the Bank of England. In contrast, M4 is known as a *broad money* definition and in general terms includes notes and coins in circulation plus current and deposit accounts of the banks, share and deposit accounts of the building societies and private sector holdings of bank and building society certificates of deposit (in all cases denominated in sterling). Figures for the official monetary aggregates published by the Bank of England and commented upon in the financial press are obtained from returns submitted by banks and other relevant financial institutions to the Bank of England. It should be noted that outside the UK, it is common for 'narrow' money to be defined in terms which correspond to M1, and 'broad' money in terms which correspond to M2 or M3.

The existence of a number of official monetary aggregates arises from the experience that no one monetary measure on its own is adequate as a predictor of change in the level of economic activity. As the monetary environment changes, a monetary aggregate which was especially relevant may no longer be so. This explains why in the UK M2 was redefined and reintroduced in 1982, why M0 was introduced for the first time in the same year, and why the definition for M4 was established in 1987. But the existence of various official measures of the money supply has its drawbacks. Notably, governments are likely to emphasize those monetary aggregates which are performing as planned while ignoring those which have not behaved so well – even when the aggregates which have misbehaved may present a more accurate picture of the impact of monetary growth upon the level of economic activity. This point is important in relation to the government's attempts to *target* monetary growth with a view to bringing down inflation.

Targeting the money supply

In March 1980 the newly-elected Conservative government in the UK unveiled its anti-inflation policy with the announcement of the first *medium-term financial strategy* (MTFS). For policy purposes, growth in a broad measure of the money supply was chosen as the main target; this was £M3 ('sterling M3'), which was broadly defined as notes, coins, sterling current and deposit accounts at UK banks and private sector holdings of sterling bank certificates of deposit (later simply called M3). However, achieving the desired growth in M3 in the ensuing years proved problematic, and indeed in 1987 the Chancellor quietly announced the end of targeting broad money in the budget of that year.

The decision to abandon the targeting of M3 came after more than a decade of increasingly unsuccessful marksmanship (see Table 6.1).

Table 6.1 Monetary targets (£M3).

Target period	Target range %	Outturn %	Overshoot from target mid-point %
4/76–4/77	9–13	17.7	+6.7
4/77–4/78	9–13	16.0	+5.0
4/78–4/79	8–12	10.9	+0.9
10/78–10/79	8–12	13.3	+3.3
6/79–4/80	7–11	10.3	+1.3
6/79–10/80	7–11	17.8	+8.8
2/80–4/81	7–11	18.5	+9.5
2/81–4/82	6–10	14.5	+6.5
2/82–4/83	8–12	11.0	+1.0
2/83–4/84	7–11	9.7	+0.7
2/84–4/85	6–10	12.2	+4.2
2/85–4/86	5–9	16.6	+9.6
2/86–4/87	11–15	19.0	+6.0

Source: Financial Statement and budget reports; Bank of England Quarterly Bulletin

Monetary targets were published initially by the Labour government from 1976, although the policy of monetary targeting reached a peak under the Conservative administration from 1979. In a speech in Autumn 1986, the governor of the Bank of England had strongly hinted that the abolition of targets for M3 was inevitable:

> Only two of the past six annual target rates of growth for M3 have been achieved and, of these two, that for 1982–3 was achieved only after the target range indicated in the previous MTFS had been raised in the 1982 budget . . . . It is . . . perfectly fair to ask whether in these circumstances a broad money target continues to serve a useful purpose . . . [and whether] we would be better to dispense with monetary targetry altogether, and I shall be considering with the Chancellor whether that point has arrived in relation to broad money when we come to review the MTFS framework.

A former eminent Bank of England economist, Charles Goodhart, has commented that once the monetary authorities try to control an economic statistic, which formerly may have had a close relationship to inflation, its behaviour changes so as to make it unsatisfactory (this phenomenon has been labelled Goodhart's law). The main reason for the authorities' inability to control the growth of M3 was the dramatic deregulation of the financial services sector in the 1980s and the consequent acceleration in the rate of financial innovation. The first step was taken in 1979, shortly after the new Conservative administration took office. It involved the abolition of foreign exchange controls which had existed since the Second World

War. This meant that there was now nothing to prevent capital freely flowing into and out of the country. The next major landmark was the passage of two Acts of Parliament in 1986 which fostered an increasingly competitive climate in the financial markets: the Financial Services Act and the Building Societies Act. These Acts led to a flood of foreign capital and foreign financial institutions into the UK and removed many of the prudential controls under which banks and building societies, in particular, had operated. At the same time, deregulation also applied to the operation of the Stock Exchange in London, which among other things opened up its membership to foreign financial institutions. The introduction of '24 hour' trading in stocks and shares further encouraged the inflow of foreign investment funds.

It is not difficult to appreciate why the government has generally failed to achieve its monetary targets in the light of the financial innovations which were taking place. For example, building societies are now able to offer virtually a full range of personal banking services, including cheque guarantees, personal loans, limited overdrafts, etc. Given that building society deposits were traditionally regarded as savings accounts, these changes have blurred the distinction between the M3 measure of the money stock which was formally targeted and the M4 measure which was not. At the same time, growth in the use of 'plastic money' and the introduction of facilities for electronically transferring funds (e.g. EFTPOS – electronic funds transfer at the point of sale) distort the predictability of any relationship between the money supply and price changes.

The extent to which the financial sector responded to deregulation in the form of new financial innovations probably took the authorities by surprise. Having abolished all direct controls on lending by banks in the previous years and with the abolition of foreign exchange controls which facilitated international borrowing, the government was left only with interest rates as the policy instrument for controlling monetary growth. The Labour opposition called for a return to direct control over bank credit in the late 1980s when interest rates soared, including the use of Bank of England directives to restrain lending. But the government continued to argue that such methods were unacceptable on philosophical and technical grounds.

On philosophical grounds the Conservative administration favoured free markets and viewed credit controls, which limited the amounts that banks were permitted to lend, as an unwarranted intrusion into private banking. The technical argument related to the openness of the UK money and capital markets. With the abolition of foreign exchange controls, alongside the other financial changes which produced more internationally integrated financial markets, the government argued that it would not be physically possible to restrict lending. Even in the 1960s, when the commercial banks were prevented from time to time by government from increasing their lending in line with the demand for credit, new quasi-banks such as hire purchase finance companies (some owned by the commercial banks) spread to fill the vacuum. Today, restrictions on credit would lead to borrowing from banks abroad. In any event, credit controls are not necessarily an alternative to high interest rates. As the interest rate is the price of borrowing money, anything which restricts the supply of credit is likely to push up interest rates.

Nevertheless, interest rates alone seem to be inadequate to restrict monetary growth sufficiently to squeeze out inflation and as such their use has been referred to as a 'blunt instrument'. There are two main reasons for this:

1. Governments are often unwilling to take the political risk involved in raising interest rates to the levels which are possibly necessary to arrest the growth in the money supply. For example, following a sharp rise in unemployment (to over three million) associated with high interest rates in the early 1980s, the UK government seemed reluctant to risk any further worsening in the state of the economy.

2. Interest rate policy may be focused more upon supporting the exchange rate than upon restraining the growth in the domestic money supply (see Chapter 9).

At the same time, the UK government appears to have become less convinced about any direct link between growth in the (broad) money supply and inflation, and policy has shifted to become more broadly based. This change of attitude is reflected in the writings of many economists in the 1980s, in that the simplistic notion of a direct link between the growth in broad money and inflation (sometimes unflatteringly referred to as *punk monetarism*) was ridiculed.

Following the demise in 1987 of M3 as the basis for monetary targeting in the UK, M0 became the only monetary aggregate for which targets were publicly announced (although the Treasury continues to monitor the growth in broad money). Instead attention switched towards maintaining the exchange rate within unpublished bands and to pursuing targets for the PSBR as a percentage of GDP. Also, although the Conservative government always recognized a link between the PSBR and the growth in the money stock, the emphasis placed upon the PSBR figures seemed to wax as the interest in money supply targets waned. Officially, today both M0 and M4 are 'monitored' rather than 'targeted'.

The growth of M0 is still monitored because of its close relationship historically with movements in money GDP. Monetarists who favour targeting this aggregate argue that it provides a good barometer of the level of economic activity. For example, when M0 is rising quickly this implies

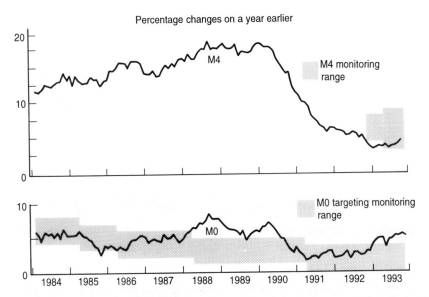

Figure 6.4 Monetary growth, M0 and M4. *Source*: HM Treasury (1993) *Financial Statement and Budget Report 1994/5*, HMSO, London, p. 53.

that economic activity (money GDP) is also rising fast. Critics of the measure, however, question whether M0 provides a useful *leading indicator* of inflation. Also, since it is made up largely of notes and coins in circulation, it is not too surprising that it rises as money GDP increases. It is not entirely clear, however, whether the causation is from M0 to money GDP or vice versa (the problem we noted earlier with regard to the relationship $MV = PT$). When economic activity is increasing, more notes and coins are used for transaction purposes. Perhaps, somewhat cynically, the government could be accused of favouring M0 as its principal measure of monetary growth simply because it is the one which has remained within or reasonably close to its prescribed target or monitoring ranges. In other words, it has generally behaved more satisfactorily than the wider definitions of the money supply such as M4 (see Figure 6.4).

Criticisms of monetarism

Just as Keynesian economics was subjected to substantial criticism in the 1970s, so too has monetarist philosophy come under scrutiny, in terms of both its theoretical foundations and its effectiveness in achieving its desired objectives.

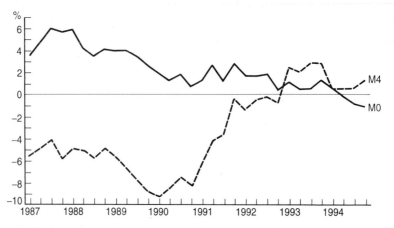

Figure 6.5 Velocity of circulation of M0 and M4: annual percentage changes.
Source: *Financial Statistics*, Table 3.1B, London, HMSO.

Monetarists' views on the importance of money are based on the quantity theory of money. In essence, this implies that there is a direct and predictable relationship between growth in the money supply and inflation. Monetarists further emphasize that, based on empirical research, the direction of this relationship is from changes in M to changes in P. This has been strongly challenged, however, and as yet there is no consensus view. Just because inflation tends to follow increases in money supply, as the monetarists' empirical results show, this does not necessarily mean that the increase in the money supply *causes* inflation.

In addition, the assumed constancy of V and T by monetarists in the quantity theory has been challenged on empirical grounds. The assumption of a constant T implies that the economy is always at full employment, but clearly this will not be the case in an economic recession. If there is substantial unemployment and the authorities choose to reflate the economy by increasing the money supply, this is likely to raise T (i.e. the volume of transactions and hence output) rather than P. Consequently, the link between changes in M and changes in P will be less predictable than argued by monetarists. Turning to the assumed constancy of V, if in practice the frequency with which each unit of money changes hands is subject to change over time, this compromises the usefulness of monetary measures in relation to counterinflationary policy. For example, in the extreme case, an increase in M could be offset totally by a decline in the speed with which money circulates in the economy (i.e. through a fall in V) so that MV and therefore PT remain unchanged. Empirically, V has changed over a number of years in the UK. Figure 6.5, for example, shows the annual percentage change in the velocity of circulation corresponding to M0 and M4 since 1987 (note that V can be calculated with respect to any monetary measure simply by calculating $V = PT/M$ for different definitions of M).

Apart from controversy regarding the assumptions underlying the monetarists' interpretation of the quantity theory, there is also controversy over the strength of two key linkages:

1. the link between changes in the money supply and changes in interest rates;
2. the link between changes in interest rates and aggregate demand (particularly investment) in the economy.

Monetarists believe that these linkages are strong, while their critics disagree. Monetarists argue that changes in the money supply have a significant effect on interest rates, assuming that interest rates are determined in a free market (it will be appreciated that the authorities can control either the quantity of money or the price of money but not both simultaneously. For example, interest rates cannot be raised to 50 per cent and people forced to borrow limitless amounts of money against their will.) This view rests on the monetarist belief that people's willingness to hold their assets in the form of money balances is relatively *insensitive* (or *inelastic*) with respect to the rate of interest, i.e. the demand for money (M_d) is relatively unresponsive to the price of money. This view is illustrated in Figure 6.6. Again, this is an area of considerable controversy which has been subject to much empirical testing and on which no consensus view has emerged. The issue seems to be one of degree, in the sense that the demand for money does appear to be interest inelastic at high real rates of interest (i.e. allowing for inflation in the cost of borrowing). If the M_d schedule is steep (inelastic) then any change in the money supply has a strong impact upon interest rate levels. This is illustrated by a leftward shift (reduction) or rightward shift (increase) in the money supply schedule, M_s. In the case of a reduction from M_{s_1} to M_{s_2}, interest rates will be pushed up from r_1 to r_2 (see Figure 6.6). It should be noted that this schedule is drawn for convenience as a vertical line, which suggests that the money supply is determined independently of interest rates. This may not be true in reality but it is not a crucial assumption in the debate.

Keynesian economists, on the other hand, dispute the idea that the demand for money is relatively insensitive to changes in interest rates. They argue, instead, that as interest rates vary then the demand to hold money balances will fluctuate sharply as people move their balances into and out of various interest-bearing assets. Keynesian economists identify government bonds as the most obvious alternative to holding money balances because they are risk free and, since they can be readily traded in

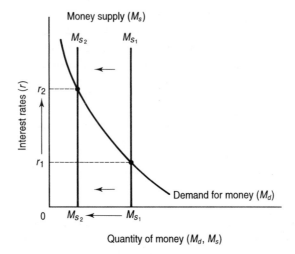

Figure 6.6 Monetarist view of the link between interest rates and changes in the money supply.

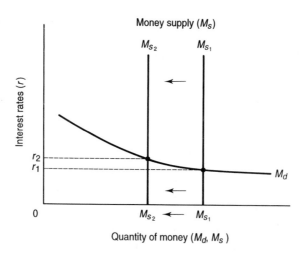

Figure 6.7 Keynesian view of the link between interest rates and changes in the money supply.

the stock market, liquid. Therefore, Keynesians argue that the willingness to hold assets in the form of money is relatively sensitive with respect to changes in interest rates on bonds: i.e. the demand to hold money balances is relatively interest elastic, as shown in Figure 6.7. If this view is correct then, in contrast to the monetarist conclusion above, measures taken by authorities to change the money supply will have little effect on the rate of interest. In Figure 6.7 a reduction in the money supply from M_{s_1} to M_{s_2} has only a small impact upon the interest rate, pushing r_1 only up to r_2.

Monetarists also hold a fundamentally different view of the likely impact of interest rate changes upon aggregate demand from that held by Keynesians. As we saw in the discussion of national income determination in Chapter 4, Keynesian economists argue that aggregate demand in general, and investment expenditure in particular, are fairly insensitive to changes in interest rates. In other words, any given change in interest rates is believed to lead to a less than proportionate change in total expenditure in the economy. The reasoning behind this is that, even if people wish to hold extra money balances (cash) as interest rates fall, these balances may not necessarily be spent on extra goods and services (i.e. on additional transactions in the economy). Instead, it is argued, these balances may be held for other purposes associated with precautionary (unforeseen contingencies) and/or speculative motives (e.g. stock market dealings).

More specifically, with regard to investment expenditure, there is no doubt that changes in interest rates have some influence upon investment decisions, but Keynesian economists argue that the relationship is unlikely to be precise. The reasons for this view are:

1. Investment expenditure in the public sector is undertaken for a host of reasons – social, political and economic – which may not be affected by the interest rate level.

2. Investment expenditure plans in the private sector commonly stretch over many years and are often large scale, so short-term changes in interest rates are unlikely to be a critical factor.

3. The key determinant of investment in the private sector is the *expected* rate of return on capital (discounted to present values) relative to the cost of raising money (the discount factor): the volatility of expectations in general will have a major effect on investment decisions, and interest rates are but one factor in determining expectations.

For these reasons Keynesians believe that even if changes in the money supply cause a significant change in interest rates, the relationship between changes in interest rates and the level of investment is unpredictable. For example, as Keynes pointed out, in an economic recession, when business expectations are depressed, reducing interest rates may not lead to more investment – he likened the use of interest rate reductions in such circumstances to 'pushing a piece of string'.

In contrast, monetarists argue that the rate of interest is a main determinant of investment decisions. The reasoning behind this view is

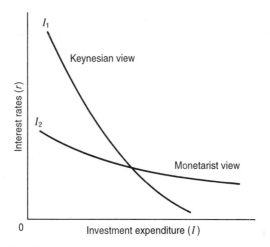

Figure 6.8 Link between interest rates and investment – Keynesian and monetarist views compared.

that a fall in interest rates will make some investments profitable, which were previously unprofitable, and therefore aggregate investment should increase (and vice versa when interest rates increase). Therefore, aggregate investment in the economy is inversely related to the rate of interest. The difference between the Keynesian and monetarist views on the impact of interest rate changes upon investment is summarized in Figure 6.8 where the curves labelled I represent levels of investment at different interest rates (referred to as *marginal efficiency of investment curves*). I_1 is a Keynesian representation where investment is not particularly affected by moderate changes in interest rates. I_2 shows the monetarist position where interest rates do have a significant effect on investment expenditure. Empirical evidence on aggregate investment seems to confirm that it has an inverse relationship with interest rates but that it is a fairly weak one and with varying time lags before investment responds. Therefore, as with the linkage between changes in the money supply and interest rates, the evidence on the effect of interest rate changes on investment is inconclusive.

Apart from these criticisms, monetarism has been questioned in terms of the effects that it has on an economy and on the practicality of implementing the measures necessary to bring about the effects desired by monetarists. This is particularly true in the context of an economy operating with considerable excess capacity. The high interest rates that may be required to bring about stable prices in an environment of high inflation may be socially and politically unacceptable as well as econom- ically damaging. Social and political acceptability is a particular problem facing democratically elected governments. Perhaps not surprisingly, some of the major success stories for monetarism in reducing inflation occurred where governments were not so vulnerable to political pressures, such as in Chile under military rule after 1973.

Moreover, it has been argued by the critics of monetarism that the economic effects of a strict monetarist strategy may be even worse than the consequences of the inflation that it seeks to remove. These suggested effects are:

1. There may be a sharp increase in unemployment as a result of deflationary monetary measures, i.e. a credit squeeze coupled with high interest rates.

2. Rising unemployment will reduce tax receipts to the government and at the same time will put increased pressure on public expenditure and the PSBR, making control of the money supply more difficult.

3. A strict monetarist approach is likely to require a reduction in the PSBR: this brings with it a conflict between economic policy and achieving a government's social objectives through expenditure on welfare programmes.

4. Monetarists emphasize the favourable effects of their policy recommendations over the longer term, but in the meantime the economic suffering may lead to a change in government and a change in economic strategy; thus any long-term benefits that might have accrued will never be realized.

5. A sharp rise in interest rates which are then held at a high level for some time may arrest investment and reduce economic growth. At the same time, in an open economy with a high degree of capital mobility, businesses may also be hampered by the effect of high interest rates on the exchange rate.

The effects of monetary policy on business

Monetarists contend that, by pursuing a policy of strictly controlling the growth in the money supply, an economic environment will eventually be created in which enterprise and efficient firms can flourish. After the credit squeeze and recession necessary to remove inflationary pressures, firms will be left 'leaner and fitter' and therefore better able to take advantage of the available opportunities which will emerge in a post-inflationary economy. Clearly, therefore, the positive effects of monetary policy on business must be looked at from a long-term perspective – and perhaps by a government with a great deal of confidence and strong nerve.

As we have intimated on several occasions in this chapter, however, monetarist measures to reduce inflationary pressures are likely to have a number of negative effects on business, at least in the short term. Possible negative effects include the impact upon exchange rates, profits, investment and even the very survival of some firms. For example:

1. High interest rates will tend to hit exporters since high interest rates attract foreign currency into the economy causing the external value of the currency to rise. Under certain circumstances this reduces the competitiveness of exports in foreign markets. At the same time, as the value of the currency rises, domestic producers suffer as imported goods gain a competitive price advantage. These effects follow since an appreciation in the foreign exchange rate makes exports more expensive in foreign markets and imports less expensive in the home market. There may, therefore, be unfavourable consequences for the balance of payments. Chapter 9 discusses the relationship between the exchange rate and the balance of payments.

2. High interest rates coupled with a high exchange rate will tend to decrease aggregate demand for domestically produced goods. This is, therefore, likely to lead to a squeeze on profits with a consequent unplanned increase in stocks of unsold goods. To finance the costs of holding these stocks, firms may have little choice but to borrow even more money despite high interest rates (this is sometimes referred to as 'distress borrowing').

3. Ultimately, firms may not be able to survive in a high interest rate and high exchange rate environment. The closure of firms has obvious implications for unemployment, investment and the future productive capacity of the economy. Some firms that shut down will be those that are the least efficient and creditworthy. At the same time, however, otherwise healthy firms may be caught out by a credit squeeze which leads to cash-flow difficulties. Firms which have committed themselves to massive investment programmes and those which are heavily dependent upon exporting are especially vulnerable to rising interest rates.

Many of the scenarios described above have been precisely those that have faced the British business community since the start of the 1980s under a Conservative government. For example, reputedly 20 per cent of UK manufacturing capacity was lost between 1979 and 1982. At the time of an appreciating exchange rate, the government adopted a high interest rate policy to reduce monetary growth. During that period, the country witnessed a record number of bankruptcies but subsequently the efficiency and competitiveness of British industry improved. A similar set of events took place between 1990 and 1992 when interest rates were maintained at a high level to support sterling's exchange rate within the European Exchange Rate Mechanism (ERM) and to reduce inflationary pressures. The economy suffered a further steep recession as a consequence.

Concluding remarks

From the late 1970s, government policy switched away from Keynesian-style demand management towards emphasis on control of the money supply. The switch was especially noticeable in the UK, where previous governments were mostly wedded to the Keynesian doctrine, but it was also evident in many other countries too. This change in stance on economic policy arose because of disillusionment with Keynesian economics during the stagflation of the 1970s. More recently, monetarism in turn has been criticized.

In part, criticism has centred upon the theoretical foundations of monetarist beliefs; in particular, whether there is a causal relationship between changes in the money stock and changes in price levels which can be predicted. In addition, monetarist policies have proved difficult to implement effectively. Finding a measure of the money supply which captures the effect of monetary changes on inflation has proved tricky, especially one which can be used with confidence and which can define desirable money supply targets which can actually be met. With the abolition of exchange controls and financial deregulation in the UK, the Conservative government felt it necessary to fall back upon manipulating interest rates to restrain the rise of credit in the economy. But high interest rates in turn have proved difficult to sustain over long periods for political and economic reasons. Moreover, from the mid-1980s to late 1992 interest rates appear to have been set more with a view to influencing the level of the exchange rate rather than with a view to constraining the growth in the money stock. It would merely be coincidental if the interest rate needed to maintain a particular exchange rate was also the right one to achieve the money supply target. Not surprisingly, interest rate policy in this context has been described as a 'blunt instrument'. The 'bluntness' of monetary policy effectiveness in the past may be explained by the fact that changes in interest rates have generally been *reactionary* measures, i.e. efforts to reduce inflation have too often been too little, too late. This may be likened to applying brakes with full force only after the car has gone out of control. With older cars this can have an obvious catastrophic outcome! Over the past few years, however, with inflation in the UK (and USA) running at historically low levels following the recession of the early 1990s, an important lesson seems to have been learned. At the time of writing, there have been five interest-rate increases in the UK (and seven in the USA) over the past twelve months, with no increase being greater than 0.5 per cent. Policy now is much more *proactive* in that efforts are being made to avoid a resurgence of inflationary pressures. This approach, using the same analogy as above, could be likened to the principle of ABS braking systems in modern cars – a little bit of pressure on the brakes, often! It is hoped that this will help the economy to avoid a repetition of the boom-bust cycle of the past decade.

7

Supply-side economics

The essence of supply-side economics

In the previous two chapters we considered the nature of Keynesian and monetarist economics. Both are concerned with macroeconomic policies to influence the level of *aggregate demand* in the economy – Keynesian economics primarily through fiscal measures and monetarism through controlling the growth in the money supply and interest rates. In recent years, however, some economists have switched their attention to the *microeconomic* factors which determine *aggregate supply*. They argue that the key to reducing unemployment and inflation lies in improving the ability of the economy to supply goods and services efficiently. In other words, unemployment will fall permanently only if British goods are competitive in world markets. Similarly, the reverse side of the 'excess aggregate demand' cause of inflation is an insufficient aggregate supply of goods and services to meet the current demand. In practice, most supply-side economists also favour a sound money policy to keep down inflation and to provide a conducive economic environment for employment and production. Therefore, while supply-side economics is distinct from monetarism in the sense that it is possible to support monetarist principles without favouring supply-side reforms (and vice versa), many monetarists may also be labelled as 'supply-siders'.

Supply-side economics as it is discussed in this chapter is fairly new, having emerged as a distinct area of policy analysis in the mid-1970s, but the idea that government economic policy should be concerned with supply as well as demand is not new. Throughout the post-war period successive governments in the UK, the USA, France, West Germany, Japan and elsewhere intervened from time to time with initiatives aimed at

119

increasing production. During this period these initiatives were grouped together under the title of *industrial policy*. Industrial policy measures were introduced to nationalize industry, raise investment, increase the supply of skilled labour, rationalize production, redistribute industry geographically, and to increase exports. In France (and with less success in the UK in the 1960s) economic activity was occasionally planned from the centre through the use of what were called *national plans*. These plans set down targets for the growth in production, exports, etc. over the following years. Also, the Ministry for International Trade and Industry (MITI) in Japan has been credited with aiding the expansion of Japanese industry since the 1950s by identifying potential markets and assisting investment programmes.

Modern supply-side economics is distinct from earlier industrial policy, however, because the emphasis is on establishing an economic environment conducive to private enterprise, rather than state planning and investment subsidies. Supply-side measures are thus aimed at creating an economic environment in which there is more incentive for individuals to work and save and for firms to invest, produce and employ. At the same time, supply-side economists tend to assume that aggregate demand will usually or always be sufficient to buy whatever the economy produces (in the sense that 'supply creates its own demand'). Therefore, the role of government should not be to 'plan' industry and demand, but to liberalize markets, reduce taxes and public spending and free-up the labour market.

A primary objective of supply-side policies is the creation of the necessary economic conditions to achieve fast economic growth, full employment and low inflation. In this chapter we look in particular at some of the policies which have been pursued to that end by governments, namely:

1. changes in labour laws to restrict the power of trade unions;
2. the reduction of taxation and the creation of greater incentives to work and invest;
3. the programme of privatization.

We begin by considering the economic theory which underlies supply-side economics.

The principles of supply-side economics

In essence, supply-side economics is concerned with increasing aggregate supply so that more demand can be accommodated without inflation. An economy's aggregate supply consists of the various amounts of total real

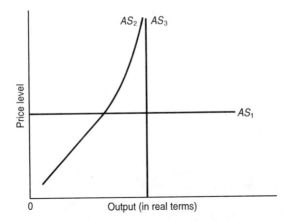

Figure 7.1 Aggregate supply schedules.

output that producers are able and willing to produce at various price levels. Therefore, an economy's aggregate supply curve reflects the relationship between the volume of production in the economy at different price levels. In principle, the aggregate supply curve can be horizontal, upward sloping or vertical, depending upon the precise relationship between rising prices and output (since producers are most unlikely to supply more at lower prices, however, the supply curve will presumably not be negatively sloped). These possible shapes are illustrated in Figure 7.1.

There is no real consensus among economists, however, about which type of aggregate supply curve is most likely. A horizontal aggregate supply curve such as AS_1 suggests that supply will increase without a rise in the price level in the economy – which implies that output can rise without unit (average) costs rising. In other words, more workers can be attracted into employment without offering higher real wages, more capital can be obtained for investment without an increase in interest rates, and an increase in the demand for raw materials and components does not cause their unit price to rise. This situation is most likely to be found where there is substantial unemployment of resources.

In contrast, an upward sloping aggregate supply curve such as AS_2 implies that higher units of output are associated with a higher price level. Higher prices may be necessary to induce firms to produce more. Also, increased output means more demand for factors of production such as labour and capital which may raise their unit price and therefore unit production costs. As the economy gets closer to Keynesian full employment (or, from a monetarist perspective, the 'natural rate of unemployment' as discussed later in this chapter) so prices are driven higher for each proportionate increase in output.

Lastly, a vertical aggregate supply curve such as AS_3 means that the volume of output (in real terms) cannot rise. Keynesians associate the vertical aggregate supply curve only with a fully employed economy (see Chapter 5), but some monetarists argue that, since workers appreciate the meaning of purchasing power, a mere increase in *money* wages does not lead to more employment and therefore output will not rise. For example, if workers are offered £10 per week more to attract them into employment or to work overtime, but this is completely offset by rising prices, then no more labour will be supplied since (real) wages will not have changed. Similarly, in so far as firms increase output in response to the lure of higher real profits, a doubling of profits alongside a doubling of prices will have no effect on their decision to supply (this 'rational' behaviour is in keeping with a branch of monetarist philosophy couched within *rational expectations theory*). Consequently, output is unaffected by (i.e. is independent of) the price level. At best, there may be only a temporary rise in output when prices rise until such time as workers and firms realize that the increases in wages and profits do not amount to real increases. In other words, until expectations about further inflation adapt to the actual price rise.

The precise nature of the aggregate supply curve is important in appraising the value of Keynesian demand management techniques for the following reason. If the aggregate supply curve is horizontal, an increase in aggregate demand resulting from an injection of government spending or a reduction in taxation will lead to more output and therefore more employment without the emergence of inflation. This is shown by the shift in aggregate demand from AD_1 to AD_2 in Figure 7.2 with the price level remaining at P_1 but output rising from Y_1 to Y_2. Even where the aggregate supply curve is upward sloping, although more demand produces some rise in prices (i.e. inflation), output and employment will still increase. In Figure 7.3 this is shown as an increase in aggregate demand from AD_1 to AD_2 with prices rising from P_1 to P_2 and output from Y_1 to Y_2. (Note that the AD line is downward sloping in the following diagrams because the price level is on the vertical axis. It is assumed that more will be demanded at lower prices.)

Both of these possibilities, therefore, imply that Keynesian demand management techniques can boost production and employment in certain circumstances. Where, however, the aggregate supply curve is vertical, more aggregate demand merely spills over into inflation with no beneficial effects on production and unemployment since supply is fixed. This is shown in Figure 7.4 as a rise in aggregate demand from AD_1 to AD_2 leading to a corresponding rise in prices from P_1 to P_2 with output remaining at Y. Therefore, in this situation Keynesian techniques are simply inflationary and do not stimulate employment. In which case, if aggregate supply does not respond to price rises, as some economists believe, how can production and employment be increased?

According to supply-side economists, the solution lies in measures which will shift the aggregate supply curve to the right (e.g. from Y_1 to Y_2)

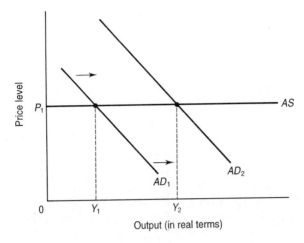

Figure 7.2 Horizontal aggregate supply schedule.

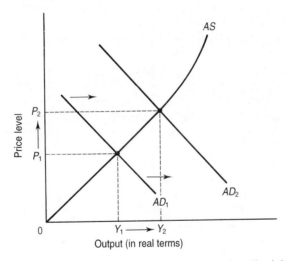

Figure 7.3 Upward sloping aggregate supply schedule.

as in Figure 7.5 (this is equivalent to shifting the production possibility curve outwards in Figure 1.2 (see page 8), meaning that potentially more of all goods and services are available). This can be achieved by either (or both) of the following:

1. increasing the availability of economic resources, i.e. more labour, capital or natural resources;

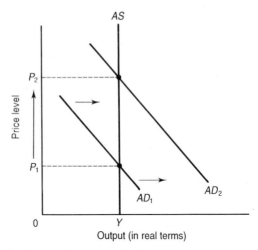

Figure 7.4 Vertical aggregate supply schedule.

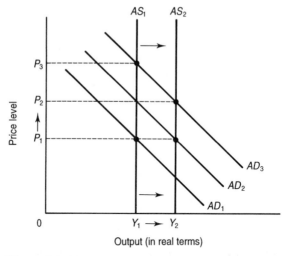

Figure 7.5 Shifting the aggregate supply schedule.

2. changes in technology and other methods of increasing the productive efficiency with which the available economic resources are used in the economy.

   Since the availability of economic resources changes slowly over time, for example as the population rises, and few changes in technology produce immediate and dramatic effects on output, it follows that shifting the aggregate supply curve to the right is a slow and continuous process. Supply-side economists argue, however, that governments can take measures to encourage the more efficient use of the existing resources and to encourage investment and technological change over the longer term.

In Figure 7.5 the aggregate supply curve is assumed vertical, though the existence of an upward sloping curve would not substantially alter the following argument. The effect of supply-side policies is to shift the curve from AS_1 to AS_2. If aggregate demand remained unchanged (AD_1), the result would be a rise in real output (from Y_1 to Y_2) alongside a fall in the price level (to below P_1). In practice, however, the purpose of shifting the aggregate supply curve is to permit aggregate demand to rise without inflation. This is illustrated by the rise in aggregate demand from AD_1 to AD_2. Note that real output has risen, from Y_1 to Y_2, but that prices have stayed constant at P_1. If aggregate demand was permitted to rise faster than aggregate supply, to AD_3, then prices would rise to P_2 but by much less than if aggregate supply had remained fixed at AS_1 (i.e. P_3).

Increasing aggregate supply, therefore, permits a higher level of demand and economic activity while suppressing inflation. This helps to explain why the study of supply-side economics has become so popular. Supply-side policies, especially when combined with a 'sound' monetary policy, appear to offer a means of tackling both inflation and low economic growth (and, consequently, rising unemployment), i.e. the problem of stagflation. Having studied the theory which lies behind supply-side economics, we now consider some specific supply-side measures adopted by the government in the UK since the early 1980s.

Supply-side economics in practice

After its election in 1979 the Conservative government largely shunned the aggregate demand management policies of previous governments in favour of supply-side policies which encouraged private enterprise. This development amounted to a profound shift in macroeconomic policy and was mirrored by similar policy changes in other countries.

The Conservative government introduced a large number of supply-side measures aimed at improving the performance of the economy by encouraging private investment. They can be grouped into three categories.

1. *Improving the flexibility of the labour market* through trade union reforms, education and training initiatives (e.g. the national curriculum and the Youth Training Scheme), housing reforms to increase the geographical mobility of labour (such as the sale of council houses to their tenants

and reform of the Rent Act), social security changes and alterations to employment protection legislation, and by removing the powers of wages councils to set minimum wages.

2. *Improving economic incentives* by reducing taxation on companies and individuals to create incentives to save, invest and work.

3. *Deregulation and privatization* of public services (e.g. bus transport) and publicly-owned industries (e.g. telecommunications, gas, water and electricity). One intended side-effect of this programme has been the introduction of wider share ownership in the UK, which the government believes is important in maintaining public support for private investment and profit-making.

In addition, the government has been a strong critic of minimum wage legislation within the European Union.

Improving the flexibility of the labour market

In a highly competitive labour market, wages should find their free-market level. This is where the demand for labour by firms equals the supply of people willing to work at a given wage rate. Once all of those wanting work at the going wage rates are employed then there is no *involuntary* unemployment (though some people may remain unemployed as they hold out for jobs offering higher wages).

No economic subject is more emotive and controversial than unemployment. Economists argue over what is the optimal unemployment rate that will maximize economic growth without spilling over into inflation. Politicians, whose task it is to choose and implement economic policy, worry also about what rate of unemployment is socially and politically acceptable. Particularly controversial is the notion of a so-called *natural rate of unemployment* (NRU), a phrase associated with free market economists.

The natural rate of unemployment is defined as that rate of unemployment which exists when the demand for labour equals the supply of labour that is willing to work at the wage rates on offer. These wage rates are the *real* (inflation-adjusted) wage rates and reflect the real cost for businesses of employing labour. Other things being equal, when real wages rise the cost of employing labour increases and so fewer people are employed. Similarly, if the real wage falls, industry will demand more labour and so more people are employed. The natural rate of unemployment is thus that rate of unemployment which an economy can expect to achieve without triggering inflationary pressures in the labour market. (The 'natural' rate is also, therefore, referred to as the non-accelerating inflation rate of unemployment NAIRU.)

The natural rate of unemployment is, therefore, associated with a particular level of *voluntary* unemployment at any particular time, reflecting the relative benefits of working and not working. It is important to note that those unemployed are not necessarily social welfare scroungers or dole cheats: they have simply made a rational economic choice not to work given the current wages on offer (relative to the cost of living) and their preference for leisure over work. Insofar as state welfare benefits make it easier to turn down low-waged jobs, however, some economists believe that a generous welfare state system raises the level of unemployment. When welfare benefits rise in real terms, the relative costs and benefits of working or not working change. More people can be expected to reject low paid jobs: they decide that they are 'better off' on the dole.

Not all economists are happy with the concept of a natural rate of unemployment. In addition others, while accepting the general idea, find difficulty in applying it. What is the market-clearing real wage at present? Can we estimate it? Does it always follow that the rate of unemployment is responsive to changes in state welfare payments? Even if it is, is cutting welfare benefits a socially or morally acceptable way of reducing unemployment? Are there better ways? These are but a few of the questions that arise in trying to address this issue.

The UK government from the early 1980s adopted a number of policies aimed at reducing involuntary unemployment by making the labour market more competitive or 'flexible'. Convinced that trade unions destroy jobs (by raising wages above the levels employers can afford if they are to remain competitive in world markets), the government introduced a series of pieces of employment and trade union legislation to curb union power, namely:

1. Employment Act, 1980. This Act restricted 'secondary' industrial action (sympathy strikes) and made picketing away from the strikers' own workplace unlawful. It also limited employees' unfair dismissal rights, restricted the enforceability of closed shop agreements and repealed certain union recognition and arbitration machinery provisions.

2. Employment Act, 1982. This legislation made unions liable for damages for unlawful industrial action, narrowed the statutory definition of a trade dispute, and further restricted the enforcement of the union closed shop.

3. Trade Union Act, 1984. This statute made industrial action unlawful without a prior strike ballot and required union executives to be elected by five-yearly secret ballots.

4. Employment Act, 1988. This legislation established a Commissioner for the Rights of Trade Union Members, to assist union members with

grievances to take legal action against their unions. It also required union postal ballots and prohibited both dismissal for non-union membership, and the disciplining by unions of members who refused to take part in an industrial action.

5. Employment Act, 1989. This Act limited rights for time off work for union duties and repealed certain laws regulating the work of young people. It also removed the legal requirement for small firms to provide written statements relating to disciplinary procedures.

6. Employment Bill, 1990. This legislation abolished the closed shop and removed legal immunity for what are known as wildcat or unofficial strikes, i.e. strikes which do not have official union backing.

7. Trade Union Reform and Employment Rights Act, 1993. This made the automatic deduction of union subscriptions unlawful.

This legislation, along with high unemployment levels throughout most of the 1980s, has reduced the number of strikes in British industry, as intended by the government. In support of its policy, the government has pointed to studies which link unions with unemployment. For example, research by Professor Patrick Minford at Liverpool University suggests that the increase in trade union militancy from the early 1960s was a direct cause of higher unemployment by pricing labour out of employment. He estimates that unions push up real wages by as much as 12 to 15 per cent above their free market levels, leading to between 400,000 and 800,000 fewer jobs. Another study by Professors Layard and Nickell of the London School of Economics, published in 1985, estimated that around 23 per cent of the rise in unemployment between 1956 and 1983 was caused by the actions of trade unions.

Although it is difficult to lay all the blame for the sharp rise in unemployment in the early 1980s and again after 1989 at the door of the unions, 'taming the unions' has nevertheless remained a key component of the government's supply-side policies. According to the government, 'real wages in the UK have not been sufficiently responsive to labour market conditions and have risen too fast' (HM Treasury, *Economic Progress Report*, October 1987). The government clearly sees the unions as being one important cause of this lack of wage responsiveness, but another factor identified was the structure of unemployment and social security benefits which evolved in the post-war period.

The extent to which unemployment benefits and other welfare payments create inflexibility in the labour market is controversial. No doubt, overgenerous payments will dull incentives among the unemployed to seek jobs. A high *replacement ratio* (the ratio of income received out of work to income received in work) will have a marked disincentive effect leading to what has been termed an *unemployment trap*. It is far from clear, however, that UK benefits are anywhere near this level. Professor Minford has been a leading advocate of the view that welfare benefits in the UK, coupled with high taxation on low incomes, have been a major disincentive to the unemployed finding work. But in 1982, the Department of Health and Social Security calculated that only around 3 per cent of the unemployed had a higher income out of work than in work, while 40 per cent had state benefits equivalent to under one-half of their in-work incomes.

Such estimates may, however, underestimate the disincentive effects of the welfare state and, in the 1980s and 1990s, the UK government has attempted to make the trade-off between the dole and work less favourable to remaining unemployed. Particular measures have included indexing social security benefits to retail prices rather than earnings (earnings have grown much more quickly than prices), reforms in social security, and making the obtaining of benefits more difficult, especially for school leavers. In addition, one of the earliest actions of the government was to subject unemployment benefits to income tax and to scrap the earnings related supplement, which provided additional unemployment benefit based on the previous level of earnings at work. These policy initiatives have helped relieve the unemployment trap so that today it appears to be a major problem only for a small minority of the unemployed.

Improving economic incentives

In addition to reforming welfare payments, the government has attempted to increase flexibility in the labour market by reducing the burden of taxation in the UK so as to make working more worthwhile. The policy of reducing taxes is also intended to act as a spur to investment and private enterprise. A main claim of supply-side economists is that high tax rates have created major disincentives to work, save and invest. This was echoed in the Chancellor of the Exchequer's March 1986 budget speech:

> Reductions in taxation motivate new business and improve incentives at work. They are the principal engine of the enterprise culture, on which our future prosperity and employment opportunities depend.

Between 1979 and 1996 the following major tax changes were introduced:

1. Reduction in the marginal rate of income tax on high incomes from 83 per cent on earned income and a penal 98 per cent on unearned income (e.g. interest and dividends) to a uniform rate of 40 per cent.
2. Reduction in the basic rate of income tax (the maximum rate paid by around 90 per cent of income tax payers) from 33 to 24 per cent (there is

also a lower rate of 20 per cent applicable to the first £3,900 of income in 1996/7).

3. Reduction in the rates of corporation tax on company profits from 52 and 40 per cent, depending upon the level of profits earned, to 33 and 24 per cent respectively.

4. Raising income tax thresholds to take more people out of tax, thereby reducing the extent of *fiscal drag* (see Chapter 5 for an explanation of fiscal drag).

5. Major technical changes to tax legislation aimed at alleviating the impact of capital gains tax and the taxation of lifetime capital transfers.

6. Tax exemptions and other incentives for investment in plant and buildings, new companies and financial securities (e.g. enterprise zones, the Business Expansion Scheme, share options, personal equity plans, etc.).

The idea that there is a significant relationship between tax rates and the willingness to work was popularized by the *Laffer curve*, reputedly conceived on the back of a restaurant table napkin by the Californian economist Professor Arthur Laffer. The basis of this concept is the belief that there is an optimal tax rate which will maximize government revenue. When the tax rate is zero there is, of course, no tax revenue. Equally, if the tax rate was set at 100 per cent, presumably tax revenue would also be zero since there would be no incentive to work or invest at all and, hence, there would be no income to tax. It follows, therefore, that somewhere between these two extreme rates there must be a tax rate which maximizes tax revenue. Although the precise shape of the Laffer curve is not entirely clear, it is conventional to draw it with a smooth slope and with one peak as in the right-hand side of Figure 7.6.

As the tax rate is increased from zero to T_1, government tax revenues rise as shown by the Laffer curve TT. Beyond T_1, however, raising tax rates is counterproductive. The disincentive effects of high taxation reduce the tax base (e.g. hours worked) so that, although the amount out of each pound earned taken in tax rises, the number of pounds earned falls more quickly and therefore less tax is recovered. In other words, if the current tax rate is above T_1, it would pay government to *reduce* the rate as tax revenues would actually rise.

Turning to the left-hand side of the diagram, the curve GG marks out the rate of growth in GDP (gross domestic product) per annum at different tax rates. Once again a single peak is assumed at G_1. Below G_1 a rise in the tax rate is associated with higher economic growth. The provision of certain public services financed from taxes, for example roads, defence and law and order, are conducive to private investment. Without them there would be insufficient security to produce and inadequate communications to

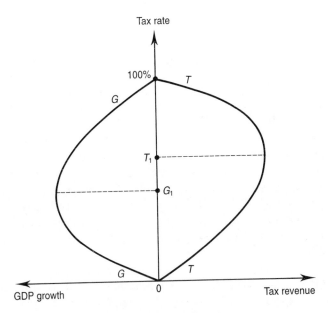

Figure 7.6 The Laffer curve.

distribute products. Beyond G_1, however, taxation and the related public spending are associated with a lower growth rate. Note that there appears to be no reason why G_1 and T_1 should be at the *same* tax rate. In other words, the rate of tax which maximizes tax revenues to government may not be the same as that which maximizes economic growth. In Figure 7.6, G_1 is below T_1, suggesting that the tax rate which maximizes the growth in GDP is less than that which provides the largest government revenue. In this case government has a choice to make between maximizing its own income and maximizing economic growth.

On the basis of this logic, Professor Michael Beenstock in 1979 predicted that by reducing the tax/GDP ratio in the UK from 40 to 35 per cent, coupled with sharp reductions in top marginal tax rates, GDP would increase by 15 per cent. This study, however, was subsequently sharply criticized on the grounds that there was no clear evidence that reducing tax rates would necessarily cause people to work harder and produce more. In a later study for the Treasury on the impact of tax cuts upon the labour supply, Professor C.V. Brown of Stirling University concluded that: 'the changes in predicted hours are very largely the effect of the change in the level of demand constraints. Little of the change in predicted hours is the result of changes in taxation.'[1] This suggests that tax cuts are likely to have a more important effect on aggregate demand, as Keynesians would predict (see Chapter 4), than on aggregate supply.

The Laffer curve is an interesting concept and useful insofar as it draws attention to the possibility that reducing tax rates might actually benefit government revenues, while at the same time boosting economic growth. It is, however, difficult to know at any given time whether a country has tax rates which put it above or below the peaks of the growth rate and tax revenue curves. Without this knowledge we cannot say what effect cutting (or increasing) tax rates will have on the level of economic activity or government income.

Some economists are sceptical of the idea that cutting tax rates really does lead to an appreciable gain in economic growth, while others are of the view that reducing taxes may not require cuts in public spending because tax revenues actually rise. In the USA and the UK in the 1980s reductions in tax rates were indeed associated with both a rise in economic growth and more government tax receipts. The causation, however, is not clear. Economists who support tax cuts point to this experience as proof of the Laffer effect. Others, however, point out that faster economic growth *produces* higher incomes, which then generate higher tax receipts, and that it is not clear that the tax rate cuts are responsible for the higher growth rate.

In assessing the likely consequences of tax changes, economists distinguish between what are called *income* and *substitution effects*. In terms of income tax, the income effect depends upon the *average rate of tax (art)*, which is equal to the tax paid (T) divided by the *tax base*, i.e. income (Y). Thus,

$$art = T/Y$$

The substitution effect, by contrast, is associated with the *marginal rate of tax (mrt)* which is equal to the change in tax paid (ΔT) divided by the change in income (ΔY). That is,

$$mrt = \Delta T/\Delta Y$$

When deciding to increase hours of work or work effort, individuals are concerned with small or marginal changes in working. Therefore, it is the *mrt* rather than the *art* which matters since this tells us what percentage of the extra income earned goes in tax. This also applies to a reduction in employment where the *mrt* determines the net of tax income forgone by not working. This means, for example, that a cut in income tax rates creates a greater incentive to work by increasing the marginal benefit of work (in terms of after-tax income), compared with the other options of leisure time or unemployment. In contrast, a cut in the income tax rate provides a disincentive to work because the amount of work needed to produce a given after-tax income is reduced. If people discover that, after the tax rate reduction, they can achieve their former income with less work than previously, they may decide to work fewer hours and take more leisure. Therefore, only if the substitution effect of a tax rate dominates the income effect will there be a net incentive to increase work effort.

Apart from identifying the existence of substitution and income effects of tax rate changes, it is difficult to deduce what overall effect a tax change will have on the incentive to work and, by similar logic, incentives to invest and save. Therefore, as in the case of the Laffer curve, we are able to conceptualize the effect of tax changes, but this does not take us much further forward in deciding in a specific case, such as the UK in the 1990s, whether reductions in taxation must necessarily increase economic activity. Neither theory nor empirical evidence based upon studies of the effect of taxation on work, investment and savings in the UK, provide strong grounds for believing that modest tax changes will lead to an appreciable improvement in economic performance. At the same time, there is equally no reason to become complacent about the effects of taxation on the economy. Presumably the logic behind the Laffer curve holds and at *some* tax rate economic growth suffers. The unanswered question is whether the UK economy prior to 1979 had tax rates which damaged the economy and, therefore, whether the reductions introduced since have improved incentives to work, save and invest resulting in higher economic growth.

Deregulation and privatization

A third major strand of the government's supply-side reforms involves measures to make markets work better by removing barriers to competition introduced by the state. Like many economists, the government believes that competition is the key to higher productive efficiency, wider consumer choice and lower prices and therefore that monopolies, particularly public sector monopolies protected by statute, should be dissolved or at least controlled. There are two main parts to this programme: one concerns introducing competition to provide services supplied previously by public sector monopolies, the other involves the transfer of state-owned assets to the private sector. Both parts often go under the title of *privatization*, but here we shall use the term deregulation to describe introducing more competition and retain the term privatization exclusively to describe the sale of state-owned assets. A related policy involves introducing more competition in the private sector through reforming monopolies and wages legislation and removing restrictive trading practices in, for example, the stock market (such as the October 1986 'Big Bang' in the UK which, among other things, opened up membership of the London Stock Exchange to foreign-owned institutions), legal services and the supply of spectacles by opticians. This latter policy is not considered further here, however. Instead, we concentrate upon deregulation and privatization affecting public sector monopolies as these have attracted most public attention.

The UK government has disappointed some economists by what they see as its failure to deregulate more markets in which public sector or former public sector monopolies operate. The main initiatives have involved opening up the supply of telecommunications equipment to private firms and deregulating express coaching and local (stage) bus transport. Previously all telecommunications equipment such as telephone receivers were supplied by British Telecom (publicly owned until November 1984). In 1981, however, the government made it possible for consumers to buy and connect up to the British Telecom network equipment from competitive suppliers. A new telecommunications system operator was licensed to compete with British Telecom, Mercury Communications. Turning to coach and bus transport, previously licences to operate routes were difficult to obtain as the licensing authorities seemed keener to preserve the services of existing operators than to encourage new ones. In 1980, however, express coaching and in 1986 local bus transport were opened up to competition. Although in some areas existing operators continue to dominate services, there is evidence that elsewhere competition has produced the expected results, especially in terms of reducing prices. This was especially noticeable in the early 1980s for express coaching when fares were cut dramatically and new facilities such as video and hostess services were introduced to win over customers.

Another area in which more competition has been introduced involves central and local government and the National Health Service (NHS). Here, the government has required departments and hospitals to put out numerous services, formerly operated by public departments, to competitive tender. To retain the work, in-house units have had to slash costs, trim overmanning and abolish entrenched restrictive working practices. In local government this was given a further impetus by the Local Government Act, 1988, which made it mandatory for all local authorities to contract competitively for the following services: refuse collection, building cleaning, catering, ground maintenance, repair and maintenance of vehicles and sport and leisure management. Further services have since been included. Academic studies suggest savings for taxpayers from competitive tendering in the public sector normally of between 5 and 20 per cent.

A desire to raise the efficiency with which goods and services are delivered has also driven the government's privatization programme, though the widening of share ownership and contributions to the financing of government spending through receipts from asset sales have been further considerations. In the main, the government has justified privatization by pointing to higher efficiency in the private sector. By 1996, business assets totalling £60bn had been transferred to the private sector.

As in the case of the disincentive effects of taxation and welfare benefits, the policy of privatization is supported more by rhetoric than hard evidence. To date, the record of the privatized industries is mixed, although it has to be recognized that privatization is still young and that it is probably too soon to draw definite conclusions. The management/worker buy-out of the National Freight Consortium in 1982 appears to have been an enormous success. When shares in the company were finally floated on the stock market in 1989 they had appreciated in value to such an extent that the average worker's investment of £600 in 1982 had grown to a staggering £44,000. In contrast, however, the profitability records since privatization of British Aerospace, Jaguar Cars and Rolls-Royce, for example, have been much less impressive. A 1988 study of twelve privatized firms concluded:

> The overall picture to emerge . . .is one of substantial change. Output and profits have grown, margins have increased, employment has declined. But the relationship of these changes to the fact of privatization is not immediately apparent from the data. The privatized industries have tended to be faster growing and more profitable, but it seems that the causation runs from growth and profitability to privatization, rather than the other way around.[2]

Some studies of public and private enterprises in other countries have found that competition is the key to higher efficiency. But if this is so, what does privatization achieve? Firms such as Jaguar and National Freight already operated in competitive markets before they were privatized. Other privatized firms such as the electricity distributors and the water authorities have retained most, if not all, of their monopoly powers. Also, the privatized monopolies now face an elaborate system of licensing with price controls and regulatory offices (e.g. the Office of Water Supply, Ofwat) which have been established to protect the consumer. Such regulation may reduce incentives to be efficient. For example, a regulated company might believe that higher profits coming from more efficiency will spark off an enquiry by the regulator into the company's pricing policy. In this case, it may decide not to pursue higher efficiency.

The government's privatization programme is criticized for paying too much attention to selling off state assets and too little to the state of competition after privatization. Therefore, it appears that, while the government's policy of deregulation may well bring major gains in efficiency, it is more difficult to believe that simply selling state assets will have similar benefits. The management of state enterprises have welcomed the transfer of their industries to the private sector to remove the dead-hand of government bureaucracy and to break free from Treasury control over borrowing for investment purposes (the so-called *external financing limits*). But the extent to which this managerial freedom will translate into long-term gains to private consumers rather than higher managerial salaries and profits for private shareholders remains unclear.

Concluding remarks

Reductions in taxation, reform of labour relations and privatization (including deregulation) have been pursued as part of a concerted policy to improve the performance of the British economy. These programmes, plus the other supply-side measures outlined at the start of this chapter, are the government's answer to the argument that the British economy was overtaxed, plagued by strikes and languishing under state bureaucracy in the 1970s. Insofar as these claims are true, then the government's reforms should lead to improved economic performance. There is some evidence that UK productivity and economic growth have generally responded, though it is not as incontrovertible as government ministers sometimes claim. It should be appreciated that tax cuts may not necessarily lead to more work effort or enterprise; that the fall in the number of days lost through strikes has partly resulted from high unemployment and may rise again if full employment returns; and that privatization without more competition may not lead to higher efficiency.

Where there is scope to improve the efficiency and performance of the economy, there is a strong case for supply-side measures. More controversial is whether the free market approach is the answer or whether a more interventionist policy (such as government-funded training and subsidies) is appropriate.

Notes

1. Brown, C.V. *et al.*, *Taxation and Family Labour Supply in Great Britain* (Dept of Economics, University of Stirling, 1987).
2. Bishop, M. and Kay, J., *Does Privatization Work? Lessons from the UK* (Centre for Business Strategy, London Business School, 1988).

8

International trade

The essence of international trade

So far we have focused largely on issues and policies relating to the domestic economy. This has involved the measurement of economic activity (national income accounting), the determination of national income (via the multiplier and accelerator effects) and the impact of various policy measures (fiscal, monetary and supply-side policies) upon the performance of the national economy. We now consider the impact of external factors upon the economy, thereby widening the analysis and understanding of the economy to include the reasons for and benefits from international trading relationships. The study of international trade has a long tradition within economics. The subject has attracted the attentions of the leading economists of the past three centuries and, to a large extent, their work on international economic problems has produced some of the most important tools of analysis used by modern economists. For example, early versions of the quantity theory of money (Chapter 6) were developed in the eighteenth century to explain the effects of gold flows linked to foreign trade on the level of domestic prices.

International economics has demanded greater attention from economists and businesses alike as the extent of world economic integration and interdependence has increased. Over the past three decades, the economies of North America, the European countries, Japan and the developing nations have become more and more dependent upon each other as sources of supply, e.g. raw materials, and as markets for goods and services. Inevitably this has meant that national governments are less able to formulate national economic objectives in isolation from the influence of activity in the rest of the world. The links between policies are even more significant in terms of the world's financial and capital markets, as witnessed every day when the reverberations on any one stock market are felt across the globe – recall how the crash of the New York Stock Exchange on 19 October 1987 ('Black Monday') swept across the world.

At the same time, the growth of international trade has allowed each participating national economy to use its resources more efficiently by concentrating production on those activities to which it is best suited and from which it gets the benefits of economies of scale. In this way, trade has raised real income in each country in the same way that specialization by an individual or firm generates greater returns. Trade is beneficial in other ways: for example, improvements in technology originating in one country are shared automatically with other countries through trade in goods embodying the technological advances. Such *technology transfer*, which is also associated with the growth of the multinational corporation, is an increasingly important vehicle for economic development today in many of the less industrialized nations.

All firms are affected either directly or indirectly by international trade. The effects of this trade are felt in many forms: competition between firms for global or national market shares, availability of imported raw materials, the price of goods, investment opportunities worldwide, capital availability, employment prospects and so on. At the same time, these effects themselves are directly influenced by other forces, not least the effect of exchange rates on trade and competitiveness. This chapter provides an overview of international trade in the context of business. In particular, we examine the gains to be obtained from international trade for individual countries and the implications for economic development and firms. In reality, of course, not all countries aspire to *free* trading relationships, in the sense of trading without state interference. The growth of protectionist policies is also strong today. Conducting international business activities necessitates a clear understanding of the different motives for various policies. Hence, we examine the arguments for and against free trade and protection in order to provide a balanced view. The net result of international trade, at the macroeconomic level, is summarized in countries' balance of payments accounts. These provide an annual summary of the flows of goods and services as well as capital between countries. The make-up of the UK balance of payments accounts is explained in detail.

The UK, at various times, has suffered from substantial deficits in its balance of payments accounts. Such deficits ultimately have implications for business activity and economic growth. Various policies are open to the government to try and arrest this problem; the main ones are identified here. Attention often focuses on the role of exchange rates to cure balance of payments deficits, but given the importance of exchange rates in international business a full analysis of their impact is reserved until

Chapter 9. We begin this chapter by explaining in formal terms why most economists believe that substantial economic gains arise from international trade.

The principle of comparative advantage – an argument for free trade

Historically, countries began to trade with each other in order to make available to consumers in one country goods which were only produced in other countries. This is an oversimplification of trade today, however, since in practice the vast majority of goods and services traded are produced in many countries across the globe. This suggests that a more fundamental explanation for international trade exists. The fact is that not all countries produce goods with the same efficiency. This gives rise to the *principle of comparative advantage*, which demonstrates that trade is potentially beneficial to the economic welfare of a country if it specializes in the production of those goods and services in which it has a comparative advantage (i.e. the greatest relative efficiency). This principle can be readily illustrated by means of a simplified numerical example, highlighting, at least in theory, the gains for all countries participating in international trade.

Suppose two countries, A and B, both produce and consume two goods, say wheat and cars. Suppose that when both countries use all of their resources efficiently to produce only wheat, country A is able to produce 1,000 tonnes and B 2,000 tonnes. If all resources are switched to car production, both A and B are able to produce 500 cars each. This information is shown in Table 8.1. If we make the simplifying assumptions that factors of production are able to move freely between the production of wheat and cars within each country and that production of both can be varied without affecting average unit costs (i.e. constant cost production exists), then the production possibility frontiers facing A and B are as shown in Figure 8.1.

Unlike the production possibility curve shown in Figure 1.2, it will be observed that the curves here are represented as straight lines. This arises from the assumption of constant cost production, introduced merely to

Table 8.1 Pre-trade output levels.

	Wheat (tonnes)		Cars
Country A	1,000	or	500
Country B	2,000	or	500
Total world output	3,000	or	1,000

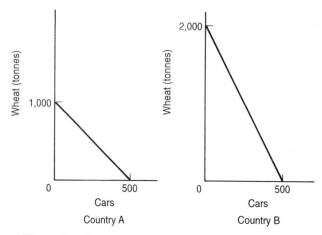

Figure 8.1 Pre-trade production possibility frontiers.

simplify the discussion. To examine whether or not there will be any gains for both countries from trading with each other, we must consider each country's *opportunity cost of production* (i.e. what it forgoes by producing one of the goods).

In the case of A, resources can be used to produce either 1,000 tonnes of wheat or 500 cars. Thus, the opportunity cost of producing one extra tonne of wheat is 0.5 of a car. Similarly for B, 2,000 tonnes of wheat or 500 cars can be produced so that the opportunity cost of producing one extra tonne of wheat is 0.25 of a car. It is clear that country B is able to produce wheat at a lower *real* cost (in terms of cars) than country A. Therefore country B is said to have a *comparative advantage* in wheat production. Conversely, if A produces one more car, the opportunity cost is 2 tonnes of wheat, while in the case of B it is 4 tonnes. Thus, A is said to have a comparative advantage in car production.

So far we have assumed that the resources in each country are devoted to either wheat or car production. Now let us assume instead that resources are divided equally to produce both wheat and cars, giving the outputs in each country as shown in Table 8.2 – with, as yet, no trade taking place between the countries.

Suppose now that an agreement to establish trading links is reached. Under what *terms of trade* will it be beneficial for both countries to agree to this trading link? Since for country A the opportunity cost of producing 1 car is 2 tonnes of wheat, then it will be happy to produce cars and exchange these for wheat provided the terms of trade exceed 2 tonnes of wheat for 1 car, i.e. provided A gets at least 2 tonnes of wheat for each car it sells. For B, the opportunity cost of producing 1 tonne of wheat is 0.25 of a car. Hence, B will be happy to produce wheat and exchange it for cars as long

Table 8.2 Pre-trade output levels without specialization of production.

	Wheat (tonnes)		Cars
Country A	500	and	250
Country B	1,000	and	250
Total world output	1,500	and	500

Table 8.3 Pre-trade output levels with specialization of production.[a]

	Wheat (tonnes)	Cars
Country A	0	500
Country B	2,000	0
Total world output	2,000	500

[a] With country A specializing in car production and country B in wheat production, based on the principle of comparative advantage.

Table 8.4 Pattern of consumption after trade.[a]

	Wheat (tonnes)		Cars
Country A	750	and	250
Country B	1,250	and	250
Total world consumption	2,000	and	500

[a] Terms of trade: 1 car = 3 tonnes of wheat

as the terms of trade are less than 4 tonnes of wheat per car, i.e. so long as the purchase of cars costs B less than 4 tonnes of wheat per car. If both countries agree to an exchange of, say, 3 tonnes of wheat per car, then both will gain by specializing and exchanging the good in which each has a comparative advantage. The outputs under specialization, before trade takes place, will now be as shown in Table 8.3.

It should be noted that the total output of wheat from A and B combined ('world output') has increased by 500 tonnes with car production unchanged, hence there has been a net gain. If A now exports 250 cars to B at an exchange rate of 1 car = 3 tonnes of wheat, then the two countries will be able to enjoy the consumption of the amounts of both goods as shown in Table 8.4.

Compared with the pre-specialization and pre-trade position shown in Table 8.2, both countries have gained in terms of additional consumption – A and B each have 250 tonnes more wheat and the same number of cars.

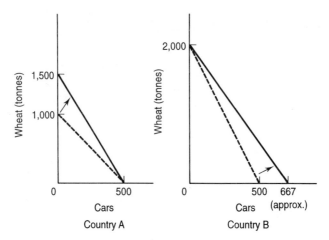

Figure 8.2 Gains from trade – post-trade production possibility frontiers.

The gains from trading can also be demonstrated by redrawing the production possibility frontiers shown in Figure 8.1 (see Figure 8.2). It will be seen that in both countries the frontiers have pivoted outwards, representing a gain in welfare. These frontiers, as before, are drawn on the basis of the amount of wheat *or* number of cars produced and consumed if specialization of production and trade takes place. For example, the 500 cars produced by A are equivalent to 1,500 tonnes of wheat (with terms of trade 1 car = 3 tonnes), while the 2,000 tonnes of wheat produced by B are equivalent to about 667 cars.

Obviously, this example, which has been used to illustrate the principle of comparative advantage and the gains from trade, has been greatly simplified. Despite this, however, it provides a useful insight into why countries should specialize in production. This applies even when they are less efficient (in absolute terms) than another country in producing every type of good. Countries should specialize in those goods in which they have a *comparative advantage*. In addition, the principle lends support to the case for free trade, i.e. trade without restrictions on imports or exports. Free trade combined with specialization results in an increase in the world's output, arising from the more efficient use of the world's resources; while this in turn has important consequences for economic development and hence for business expansion.

Further arguments for free trade

The principle of comparative advantage outlined above is the central argument used in support of free trading relationships between countries.

As noted in the introduction to this chapter, however, there are other supportive arguments:

1. International trade, by creating larger markets for goods and services, benefits business through economies of scale in production (this particular argument is central to the principle of free trade within the development of the Single European Market).
2. International trade, devoid of restrictions, is likely to increase competition between producers, thereby helping to ensure that markets are not dominated by any single producer and that consumers get the best possible deal, not only in terms of price but also in terms of choice (e.g. product differentiation).
3. Competition in world markets encourages more efficient use of the world's scarce resources.
4. International trading links are likely to foster greater economic and political co-operation between nations with implications for world peace and stability (again, the European Union is illustrative of this advantage).

Protectionism in international trade

Although the arguments in favour of free international trading relationships are powerful, countries sometimes adopt measures to restrict international trade. In this section we describe the most common forms of trade barrier and assess the arguments put forward in favour of protecting domestic industries from imports or providing some sort of state assistance, either directly or indirectly, to exporters.

Forms of trade restrictions

Trade restrictions can be applied by governments in a variety of ways, some of which may be openly identified while others may be 'hidden'. Restrictions may be categorized as follows:

1. embargoes on imports;
2. quotas on imports;
3. tariffs or customs duties;
4. other import restrictions;
5. subsidies for domestic producers and exporters;

6. exchange controls;

7. exchange rate policy.

Embargoes on imports

These are the most extreme form of restriction on international trade, representing a total ban on the importation of certain types of goods or all goods from a particular country (such as the prohibition on goods from South Africa imposed by many Commonwealth countries until the ending of apartheid in 1994). The motives are often political, frequently as a defensive or retaliatory action against another country (for example, as in the case of the UK and Argentina following the Falklands War in 1982). From an economic viewpoint, embargoes deprive consumers of choice and industry ends by paying more for its raw materials, investment goods and components. The principle of trade according to comparative advantage is undermined and the overall result is likely to be a lower rate of economic development.

Quotas on imports

These are volume restrictions on imports whereby specific limits are set on the quantity of particular products that can be imported from one or more countries. However, while the immediate effect is to limit the volume of imported goods, domestic consumers face a limited supply which, if demand is strong, tends to force up the price of affected imports (and domestic alternatives), resulting in higher profits for the producer or seller. This has indeed been the experience with Japanese cars affected by 'voluntary' quotas (see below) sold in Britain with distributors often in the position of being able to sell at full retail price with little or no discount to customers. Similarly, US restrictions on microchip imports from Japan in the late 1980s served mainly to support the profit margins of the Japanese producers being squeezed by overproduction. American computer manufacturers lost out through higher prices for a basic component.

Tariffs or customs duties

These are taxes on imported goods which have the effect of raising the selling price to the domestic consumer with the tariff revenue going to the government (instead of to the seller as occurs with quotas when prices are raised). Tariffs may be *specific* (i.e. lump sum) in nature, or *ad valorem* (i.e. proportional to the value of the good). As with quotas, they can be applied to individual goods from individual countries or they can be applied more generally. The aim of tariffs is generally to discourage domestic residents from consuming particular imported goods by raising their price (though from the government's standpoint, the additional tax revenue may be an added incentive).

Other import restrictions
Apart from tariffs and quotas, governments may restrict the flow of certain imports by imposing a whole range of complex import regulations and documentation. Excessively high safety standards may be demanded of imported goods or just sheer bureaucracy may be used to slow down the volume of goods coming into the country. For example, exporters to Japan have criticized the Japanese authorities for what is believed to be unnecessary delays in processing import documentation.

In the more difficult trading conditions since the 1970s many countries have also turned to 'voluntary' import restrictions. Tariffs and quotas often conflict with international trading agreements, notably the *General Agreement on Tariffs and Trade* (GATT) which exists to extend free trade. The UK was an initial signatory to the agreement in 1947. Voluntary controls on trade, however, subvert the spirit of the agreement without contravening its terms. The main victim of these controls has been Japan which has felt obliged, in the face of its growing balance of trade surplus with other leading industrial countries, to accept voluntary curbs on its exports. In particular, and as mentioned above, since the 1970s a voluntary quota has applied to the importation of Japanese cars into Britain. This has effectively limited the share of all Japanese manufacturers to below 11 per cent of the UK new car market. It should be noted that following completion of the Uruguay Round of GATT talks and the establishment of the new World Trade Organization (WTO) in 1995, major changes in world trading agreements are set to take place in the 1990s, including the end of voluntary export agreements. The WTO, which will take over the work of GATT, has wider powers than the GATT secretariat to police international trading practices and arrangements.

Subsidies
By subsidizing the production of goods for domestic consumption as well as goods for export, governments attempt to maintain or increase the competitive position of domestic firms in the marketplace. Subsidies may be clearly identified (for example, regional development grants and investment incentives) or they may be hidden (such as relaxed planning restrictions). Exporters may be supported by government-backed guarantees against bad debts for overseas sales and may even receive direct financial assistance. All such forms of subsidy ultimately help to lower the price of goods produced by domestic firms and hence reduce competition

from imports and assist exporters. This only applies, however, provided other countries do not adopt similar practices. Often, in fact, they do – which means that overall international trade may be little affected, while tax payers subsidize firms which benefit from higher profit margins.

Exchange controls

Governments may exercise control over the importation of certain commodities by imposing exchange control regulations. For example, exchange controls may limit the use of a country's foreign currency reserves to the importation of 'essential' goods and services only, thereby in effect blocking the importation of 'luxury' or non-essential goods (this policy is commonly adopted by developing countries to economize on the use of foreign reserves). Exchange controls may also be implemented in order to stem the flow of investment capital from a country, as in the case of the UK from the Second World War to their abolition in 1979.

Exchange rate policy

Perhaps less obvious than the methods above, a government may attempt to influence trade flows by devaluing its currency, thereby making imports more expensive in domestic markets while making its exports more attractive to foreigners. Such a policy is described as a *competitive devaluation*. Clearly, the extent to which the policy will be successful in stemming the flow of imports and boosting exports depends, among other things, on the sensitivity (*elasticity*) of demand for exports and imports to changes in their price and the extent to which the devaluation is unilateral. If two countries devalue their currencies by the same amount against each other, relative prices will remain unchanged. At the same time, the rise in the domestic price of imports will have an adverse effect on domestic production costs (imported raw materials and components cost more) leading to a rise in the general rate of inflation. This is an issue which we explore further in the next chapter.

Arguments in favour of protectionism

The arguments in favour of protectionism generally fall under one of the following headings:

1. protection of infant industries;
2. protection against 'unfair' competition;
3. support for declining industries;

4. support for strategic industries;

5. retaliation;

6. correction of balance of payments problems.

It should be appreciated, however, that the forces pressing for protectionism – producers and trade unions – are more likely to be motivated by self-interest than the public interest. At the same time, consumers who lose out from protectionism, through restricted choice and higher prices, are usually less well organized and vocal. Protectionism can therefore increase because of the power of vested interests – vested interests who attempt to justify their action in terms of the arguments below.

Protection of infant industries

It is sometimes argued that industries in the early stages of development need protection from competition in order that they can grow to a stage at which they can compete on equal terms with other countries' industries. This type of argument is generally accepted by economists as a valid reason for some of the restrictive measures described above, especially for new industries in developing economies. There is, however, a real danger that protecting infant industries makes them overreliant on state support, leading to sluggishness and inefficiency. Hence, the protection becomes permanent and the infant industry never matures. Equally, industries may be established behind tariff walls in countries where they have no long-term comparative advantage. Consequently, economic development becomes distorted and scarce resources are wasted.

Protection against 'unfair' competition

Producers often complain about unfair competition from firms in low-cost labour countries or because of subsidies granted to foreign producers by their governments. One particular form of unfair competition which attracted much attention in the 1970s and 1980s involves *dumping*, defined as the selling of goods abroad at 'uneconomically low' prices or below their production costs. The Americans and the Japanese clashed on this issue with regard to the importation of Japanese microchips into the USA in the mid-1980s, resulting in a spate of retaliatory measures (such as the temporary doubling of import duty on Japanese electrical goods into the USA).

At the same time, of course, dumping results in domestic consumers paying lower prices for the goods that are being imported, though this benefit should be weighed against the loss of jobs in domestic industries unable to compete with these lower prices. Therefore, the issue of dumping, like the issue of importing from cheap labour sources, largely becomes a question of balancing the effects on domestic employment and domestic prices. In practice, this involves not simply a cool economic evaluation of costs and benefits, but politicians deciding whether or not protectionist measures are politically acceptable to the electorate. It should also be appreciated that, from an economic perspective, cheap labour countries *should* specialize in producing goods which need abundant low-cost labour, for that is where their comparative advantage lies. This may be bad news for the textile industry in Western Europe and the USA, for example, but the resources tied up in this industry (currently protected by a quota system under the Multinational Fiber Agreement within GATT) would probably earn a higher return utilized in the production of other goods and services.

Support for declining industries

Just as a rationale for protectionist measures is support for newly established industries, so protection is also proposed to ease the burden associated with declining industries (such as steel, coal, shipbuilding, etc. in the EU during the past twenty years). Most economists would argue, however, that protection in these circumstances should be short-lived since otherwise it arrests the decline of industries in accordance with changes in comparative cost advantages in production. Also, protection reduces the incentive to restructure and become more efficient to survive. Arguably, protection should be directed at easing the burden of adjustment associated with unemployment (especially regionally concentrated unemployment) while assisting the switching of resources into new industries and skills over a longer period of time.

Support for strategic industries

Certain industries, such as defence and aerospace, may be classified as being of strategic importance from a military perspective. Also, certain high-tech industries are sometimes classified as strategic because they are perceived to be of long-term importance in a country's economic development. Consequently, protectionist measures may be adopted to safeguard the future of such industries even if there are no immediate short-term benefits to be derived. This argument, however, contains many dangers, not least who decides what is a strategically important industry? In the early 1970s, UK toy producers called for protection from imports citing strategic arguments. They argued that the industry's production processes could be readily switched to munitions in wartime. Perhaps not surprisingly, the government at the time was unimpressed. Moreover, if a high-tech industry really is vital to a country's economic development, it would surely be expected to flourish in a free market.

Retaliation

An obvious argument in support of protectionism is that of retaliation against protectionist measures imposed by another country. The danger here, however, is a rapid escalation of protectionism on such a scale that world trade is curtailed – with severe consequences for world economic development. It would be much better if the countries concerned could find a way of dismantling the existing protectionist barriers rather than adopting self-defeating retaliatory measures.

Correction of balance of payments problems

Protectionist policies are often seen as a quick and easy means for a country to reduce its balance of trade deficit. Embargoes or quotas will be immediate in their effect, while tariffs or currency devaluation are likely to take time to reduce domestic demand for imported goods – the ultimate success of these measures being dependent on the responsiveness of demand to relative price changes (see Chapter 9).

The balance of payments

As has already been argued, international trade based on the principle of comparative advantage can be beneficial to all countries that take part in it. However, even armed with protectionist measures, international trade can present countries with balance of payments difficulties arising from a persistent mismatch in the flow of exports and imports. Countries with persistently large balance of payments deficits are likely to see their economic growth slow down as part of their national income flows to other countries, unless internally generated growth can compensate for this. At the same time, those countries with persistently large balance of payments surpluses, representing net injections into the circular flow of national income, may overheat as their economies reach capacity limits, unless new capacity can be developed or part of the surplus is invested overseas (a strategy that has been followed by the Japanese through their huge investments in Europe, North America and many parts of the Far East). Furthermore, deficit countries are likely to experience a decline in the external value of their currency, while surplus countries are likely to experience a rise, both effects having important consequences for the flow of goods and services internationally. Clearly, the dynamics of international trade flows is a complex subject and we can but touch on the key issues here. We look first at the meaning of balance of payments.

The balance of payments is a summarized statement of a country's international trade transactions in goods and services and capital transactions with all other countries combined over a period of time. In the mid-1980s, some changes in the style of presentation were made to the UK's balance of payments accounts. The latest version is presented here though we comment in passing on the changes that were made.

The UK's balance of payments account is broadly divided into two parts covering:

1. current account transactions;
2. changes in external assets and liabilities (formerly referred to as capital account transactions and including changes in official foreign currency reserves and borrowings).

By definition, the sum of these two parts of the balance of payments must be equal to zero (the overall balance of payments always balances). For example, a surplus of imports over exports might be financed by a reduction in official reserves or by international borrowing; in other words, by a fall in external assets or a rise in external liabilities. Similarly, a surplus of exports over imports might lead to a rise in foreign currency reserves, new overseas investments or a repayment of past borrowings, leading to a rise in external assets or a fall in external liabilities. Media reports of a balance of payments deficit or surplus, therefore, should be clarified: they refer only to the situation on the *current account*. It is this part which reflects the difference between the value of goods and services imported and exported by the country during a given time period.

Current account transactions

The current account is subdivided for reporting purposes into transactions involving goods (denoted as *visibles*) and transactions involving services (*invisibles*). The visible balance is thus the difference between the value of exported *goods* from the country and the value of *goods* imported into the country, and is referred to as the *balance of trade*. The invisible balance consists of the sale and purchase of services between the UK and other countries, plus interest, profits and dividends received or paid, and other transfers. In more detail:

1. *Services*. These include transport services (such as shipping and aviation), banking services and other financial services (such as insurance) as well as estimated net receipts from tourism.

2. *Interest, profits and dividends.* These represent income receipts which arise from assets owned by UK firms in foreign countries (as well as payments to foreigners arising from their ownership of assets in the UK). These assets may be in the form of direct investments in companies overseas, stocks and shares held as securities overseas as well as interest earned on lending abroad by banks.

3. *Transfers.* These represent the transfer of funds to other countries (or the receipt of funds from other countries), for non-trading and non-commercial transactions. They include private gifts and grants, subscriptions to or receipts from international organizations (such as the EU) as well as government payments to developing countries and for overseas military commitments, and certain other public and private sector international currency transfers.

External assets and liabilities

The other part of the UK's balance of payments account, comprising changes in external assets and liabilities over a given time period, is subdivided as follows:

1. *Changes in external assets.* These cover resident holdings of foreign currency or shares and other investments in overseas companies and government stock by UK residents, plus loans by UK banks to overseas borrowers.

2. *Changes in external liabilities.* These cover all investments in the UK by overseas residents as well as borrowing from abroad by anyone in the UK.

It should be noted that while the assets and liabilities are recorded in the *external* (formerly capital) account of the balance of payments for the period during which they have arisen, any eventual income or payment stream in the form of interest, profits and dividends appears under 'invisibles' on the current account. It is important to appreciate this point as it highlights the 'cost', for example, in terms of potential outflows on the current account in future years arising from foreign capital inflows today, as well as the potential future inflows from investments overseas made today. Following the abolition of foreign exchange controls, annual UK portfolio and direct investments overseas rose sharply to £58bn in 1989, confirming the UK as one of the world's largest overseas investors along with Japan and the USA.

Table 8.5 shows the UK balance of payments account, based on the structure described above, for the selected years 1986, 1989 and 1992. It should be noted that in the external assets and liabilities section, one item not mentioned so far is included, namely *official reserves.*

Table 8.5 The UK balance of payments accounts.

	£ million		
	1986	1989	1992
Current account			
Visible trade			
Exports	72 627	92 154	107 047
Imports	82 186	116 837	120 453
Visible balance	−9 559	−24 683	−13 406
Invisible balance	8 688	2 171	4 786
of which			
Services balance	6 223	3 361	4 069
Interest, profits and dividends balance	4 622	3 388	5 777
Transfers balance	−2 157	−4 578	−5 060
A. Current account balance	**−871**	**−22 512**	**−8 620**
Transactions in external assets and liabilities			
Investment overseas by UK residents			
Direct	−11 649	−21 503	−9 424
Portfolio	−22 542	−36 341	−32 818
Total UK investment overseas	−34 191	−57 844	−42 242
Investment in the United Kingdom by overseas residents			
Direct	5 837	18 567	10 343
Portfolio	12 081	16 079	21 390
Total overseas investment in the UK	17 918	34 646	31 733
Foreign currency lending abroad by UK banks	−47 876	−25 688	−14 995
Foreign currency borrowing abroad by UK banks	61 366	32 384	21 460
Net foreign currency transactions of UK banks	13 490	6 696	6 465
Sterling lending abroad by UK banks	−5 838	−2 923	−10 842
Sterling borrowing and deposit liabilities abroad of UK banks	5 502	12 470	2 840
Net sterling transactions of UK banks	−336	9 547	−8 002
Deposits with and lending to banks abroad by the UK non-bank private sector	−3 094	−9 553	−7 871
Borrowing from banks abroad by:			
UK non-bank private sector	3 816	7 934	8 018
Public corporations	−31	−1 726	−506
General government	100	529	993
Official reserves (additions to −, drawings on +)	−2 891	5 440	1 406
Other external assets of:			
UK non-bank private sector and Public corporations	1 909	1 352	−9 749
General government	−509	−873	−682

Table 8.5 Continued

Other external liabilities of:			
UK non-bank private sector and			
Public corporations	568	20 975	31 319
General government	77	2 293	−2 562
B. Net transactions in assets and liabilities	−3 173	19 415	8 319
C. Balancing item	4 044	3 097	301
TOTAL BALANCE: A + B + C	0	0	0

Source: CSO (1994), *Annual Abstract of Statistics* (London: HMSO)

Transactions in official reserves

Transactions in official reserves consist of drawings on or additions to the country's official reserves (mainly gold and convertible foreign currencies), held by the Bank of England (and recorded in the *Exchange Equalization Account*). Traditionally, changes in these reserves were given prominence in the balance of payments statistics but nowadays less emphasis is placed on any changes. This has occurred because other international capital transactions have grown so dramatically in the last twenty years or so and are now, by value, extremely large in comparison.

Balancing item

The bottom line of Table 8.5 reports a balancing item. This relates to discrepancies between the total value of recorded transactions and the actual flow of money, i.e. it is the total of errors and omissions arising within the balance of payments accounts. Its value is known because the Bank of England's records show the net result of all foreign currency transactions. A positive value indicates that there have been unrecorded net inflows and a negative figure that there have been unrecorded net outflows. The size of the balancing item for any one year (as shown in Table 8.5) can be large, highlighting the difficulties in interpreting the data for any single period. Indeed, it is probably fair to say that no other national income data are subject to errors as large as those involving the balance of payments.

Management of current account imbalances

We now turn to the consequences for a country that is experiencing a persistent balance of payments deficit or surplus and consider briefly what actions can be taken to correct the imbalance. This discussion provides a natural introduction to the analysis of exchange rates in the next chapter.

An imbalance with regard to the balance of payments will have the following implications. In the case of a deficit, the country will face a drain on its foreign currency reserves and is likely to find itself getting more and more into debt with overseas monetary authorities (recall the experience of the UK in 1976 when, following several years of huge deficits, the then Chancellor Denis Healey went 'cap in hand' to the IMF to borrow funds to cover the UK debt position). This type of situation cannot, of course, persist indefinitely since both reserves and sources of borrowing are, ultimately, limited. In contrast, a country experiencing a continuous balance of payments surplus will be accumulating reserves at the expense of deficit countries. Consequently, it may be experiencing inflationary pressures in its domestic economy as the net inflow of currency boosts the domestic money supply (foreign currency inflows will ultimately be converted into domestic currency) though these may be stabilized by government debt sales (open market operations to soak up the excess money supply – see Chapter 6).

As we mentioned earlier, a deficit on the balance of payments will also tend to exert downward pressure on the country's exchange rate while a surplus will exert upward pressure. Whether or not the authorities permit the exchange rate to change at all and, if so, by how much, depends on the particular exchange rate policy that is being pursued (see Chapter 9).

Given these consequences of balance of payments imbalances, there are four possible courses of action that governments can take to correct them. (Any or all of these courses could be implemented to varying degrees at the same time.) They are:

1. protectionist measures;
2. demand management policies;
3. supply-side policies;
4. exchange rate management policies.

Protectionist measures, along with the arguments in favour and against, were discussed earlier in this chapter. Demand management policies could involve contractionary fiscal or monetary policies to reduce overall aggregate demand, including the demand for imports in the case of a balance of payments deficit. These contractionary measures could also reduce domestic inflationary pressures, thereby increasing the competitiveness of exports in world markets. On the other hand, a current account surplus could be reversed by pursuing expansionary fiscal and monetary policy measures, drawing in imports at a faster rate than the growth in exports. Broadly, if a country's rate of economic growth is faster than the average growth rate in its export markets then this will tend to cause imports to rise faster than exports through the *absorption effect* (the economy 'absorbs' more imports). In either of these situations, however, a conflict of macroeconomic objectives may well arise. For example, while deflationary measures may lead to an improvement in the current account deficit position, this may be achieved at the expense of high unemployment and lower economic growth as aggregate demand slows down. Similarly, expansionary measures to reduce a current account surplus may stimulate inflationary pressures. Ultimately, the difficult choice of which objective takes priority – the balance of payments or the domestic economic environment – is decided by government.

As we saw in Chapter 7, supply-side policies are aimed at increasing the nation's output through greater productivity and other efficiency measures. It might be the case that a current account deficit has arisen because of a lack of competitiveness on the part of domestic firms in the world marketplace, resulting in a falling demand for exports and a rising demand for imports which substitute for inferior or more expensive domestic goods. This is a view commonly put forward to explain the repeated current account deficits experienced by the UK and USA throughout most of the 1970s and again from the mid-1980s. Supply-side reforms may reverse this trend, though the process is likely to take many years. In the meantime, competitors are unlikely to be standing still.

Lastly, a current account deficit might be tackled by devaluing the currency against the currencies of international competitors. If the currency is 'managed' by the authorities (see Chapter 9), then they may engineer a devaluation. Alternatively, if the currency is allowed to float freely in the foreign exchange markets, so that its value depends entirely on the forces of demand and supply, it will decline automatically provided the supply of the currency being traded in the markets exceeds the demand for it. In the same way, the currency could be formally revalued or appreciate in the market when a country has a balance of payments surplus. It should be noted, however, that movements in the value of a currency are affected by factors other than trade flows, most notably by changes in external assets and liabilities brought about by short-term speculative movements of capital in and out of the country and longer-term flows in international investment. Therefore, there is no guarantee that a freely floating currency will lead to a balance on current account, as we see in the next chapter.

Concluding remarks

All businesses are affected by international trade whether directly, by being involved in importing and exporting, or indirectly because of the impact that the balance of payments has upon domestic economic activity.

One question which might run through a reader's mind at the end of this chapter is whether a current account imbalance matters.

There is no simple answer to this question, much depends upon what is happening to capital flows. Sustained imbalances in trade flows, unless offset by flows of capital, must eventually trigger changes in policy. If a country has a current account deficit which is financed by an inflow of investment funds from abroad then the imbalance is sustainable, especially if the capital inflow is long-term investment (short-term investment is much more of a problem because it can quickly flow out again – what is called a flight of *hot money*, precipitating a currency crisis). The USA in the latter part of the nineteenth century ran current account deficits financed by inflows of capital (from Britain and elsewhere) which went, for example, into building America's railroads. Similarly, Japan maintained its large export surplus in the 1980s, without causing an even larger rise in the value of the yen against other currencies than took place, by investing large amounts of its surplus international earnings abroad.

One issue which we have explored at some length in this chapter has been the protection of domestic producers from imports. Not surprisingly, those working and investing in industries directly threatened by imports tend to favour protectionism. On the other hand, and as we have seen, protectionism imposes major costs on consumers when they are denied access to cheaper and superior imports. Also, it can lead to inefficiency as competitive pressures are reduced. Most economists agree that competition is the key to high efficiency.

9

Exchange rate policy

The essence of exchange rate policy

The previous chapter considered the importance of international trade in business and economic development and showed how trade and capital flows give rise to a country's balance of payments account. At the end of the chapter a number of problems associated with deficits or surpluses in the balance of payments were identified along with possible solutions. We now turn to study the last of these solutions: changing the exchange rate.

The need for exchange rates arises because one country's currency is usually not acceptable as a medium of exchange in another. For example, a British exporter will want to be paid for his goods in sterling because his workers and suppliers are unlikely to accept foreign currency. The foreign buyer will therefore have to obtain sterling in order to pay for the British goods, offering his own currency in exchange. Alternatively, the British exporter may accept the foreign currency but will then convert it into sterling. The same process occurs, in reverse, when British firms import goods from overseas. Also, today, much trade in the world takes place in a third currency, notably the US dollar which in effect acts as a go-between for the exporter's and importer's currencies.

International trading relationships therefore result in a demand for and supply of currencies. This in turn has led to the development of sophisticated foreign exchange markets, for example in New York, Tokyo and London, to co-ordinate the millions of interactions of demand and supply decisions that take place every day, leading to the determination of exchange rates between currencies. Not all currencies, however, are freely exchangeable (convertible) with other currencies. Non-convertible currencies (for example the Russian rouble) are sometimes referred to as soft currencies as opposed to the hard currencies of the major Western countries.

There are many types of exchange rate policy which countries can adopt: the choice will be determined by the nature of the economic stance taken by governments and the problems faced. In essence, the policies may be categorized under three headings:

1. a floating exchange rate system;
2. a fixed exchange rate system;
3. a managed exchange rate system.

In this chapter we describe the mechanics of each system and discuss the case for each in terms of its viability and effectiveness. The choice of exchange rate system is a major issue in economics today given the degree of international integration which has evolved in recent years. Exchange rates have obvious and important implications for businesses, especially those involved in exporting and importing. It is important, therefore, that managers appreciate not only how exchange rates are determined but their impact on the macroeconomic environment in which businesses operate. Hence, in this chapter we also discuss the role of exchange rate policy in the correction of balance of payments imbalances and conclude by considering how managers can attempt to minimize the effects of changes in exchange rates on their business.

Exchange rate systems

Floating exchange rates

Under a floating system, a country's exchange rate is determined solely by the demand for and supply of its currency in the international foreign exchange markets. In other words, it is determined just like the price of any good or service in a free market. A floating exchange rate system, by definition, therefore, results in an *equilibrium* rate of exchange which will vary continuously as demand and supply forces change. When a currency's exchange value rises as a result of market forces, the exchange rate is said to *appreciate*; when its value falls it is said to *depreciate*.

The process by which currencies float up or down is illustrated in Figure 9.1. In Figure 9.1(a) the initial equilibrium exchange rate for sterling in terms of the US dollar is shown as $1.65 and arises from foreign exchange transactions totalling £Q_1. Suppose now that the demand for sterling rises as a result of an increased demand for British exports. This is shown as a shift in the demand schedule for sterling from D_1D_1 to D_2D_2. Consequently, sterling appreciates from $1.65 to $1.80 as the amount of

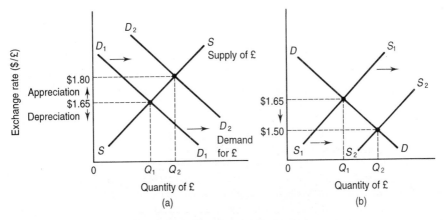

Figure 9.1 Floating exchange rates.

sterling exchanged increases to £Q_2, everything else being equal. It will be appreciated that had the demand for sterling fallen, say, due to a decline in British exports, this would have caused the demand schedule for sterling to shift to the left leading to a decline in the $/£ exchange rate.

In Figure 9.1(b), again the initial exchange rate is $1.65 but this time there is an increase in the supply of sterling, from S_1S_1 to S_2S_2, on the foreign exchange markets. This could arise, for example, if there was an increase in British demand for foreign goods. Everything else being equal, the $/£ exchange rate will depreciate to $1.50. Once again, it should be recognized that a reduction in the supply of sterling on the foreign exchanges would have led to an appreciation in sterling's value.

The above analysis of the determination of exchange rates is based upon the assumption that there is no government intervention in the foreign exchange markets. The methods by which governments can intervene are discussed below with reference to *fixed* and *managed* exchange rate systems. In other words, we have been concerned with *pure* or *free* floating exchange rates. Also, we have linked movements in exchange rates solely to changes in the demand for and supply of exports and imports. In practice, however, exchange rates are determined by a whole range of factors, as discussed on pages 169–72.

Fixed exchange rates

At the other extreme to a free floating exchange rate system lie fixed exchange rates. A government may pursue a policy of keeping the external value of its currency fixed at a stable rate by intervening in the foreign exchange markets. This intervention is carried out using official reserves to balance the demand for and the supply of the currency in order to maintain

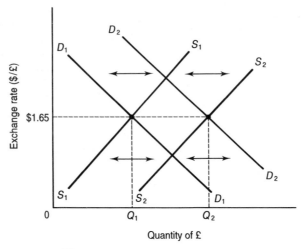

Figure 9.2 Fixed exchange rates.

the particular exchange rate at a given level. For example, as illustrated in Figure 9.2, an increase in the demand for sterling from D_1D_1 to D_2D_2 could be offset by the authorities augmenting the supply of sterling from S_1S_1 to S_2S_2 (to buy dollars for example) in the foreign exchange markets, in order to counteract the upward pressure on the value of sterling. Conversely, as can also be seen in Figure 9.2, a decrease in the demand for sterling from D_2D_2 to D_1D_1 could be offset by the authorities by, for example, restricting the supply of sterling to the market from S_2S_2 to S_1S_1. The end result of both of these actions is that the value of sterling is held at the fixed exchange rate of $1.65.

The maintenance of fixed exchange rates in the manner just described requires that the authorities hold sufficient reserves or have access to sufficient loans for intervention purposes. In the UK the responsibility for intervening in the foreign exchange market lies with the Bank of England which manages the country's foreign reserves under the guidance of the Treasury.

The gold standard
During this century there have been two periods in which fixed exchange rate systems have prevailed in the world economy. The first lasted in one form or another up until the early 1930s and was known as the *gold standard*. Under this system the value of each currency was fixed in terms of an amount of gold. This necessarily meant that the value of any particular currency was fixed in terms of any other currency. In addition, international trade was primarily financed by gold shipments and the internal money supply was broadly determined by the amount of gold held by

central banks. Basically, therefore, when exports exceeded imports, more gold flowed into the country than out. Consequently, the internal money supply rose, which in turn led to upward pressure on prices (see Chapter 6 and the quantity theory of money for a discussion of the link between the money supply and prices), which in turn caused exports to become less competitive and imports more so. This process would continue until exports equalled imports and the gold inflow, therefore, ended. A similar mechanism operated in reverse when imports exceeded exports: gold would flow out of the country, the money supply would contract and prices would fall until, again, exports and imports were in balance.

It must be stressed that this is only a brief summary of the principles of the gold standard. In practice, occasional devaluations of currency values against gold occurred and central banks did intervene from time to time to ameliorate the economic effects of gold flows. Nevertheless, up until the outbreak of the First World War the gold standard permitted a high degree of automatic balance of payments correction. It broke down in the inter-war years, however, largely because, with the growth of trade unions and large firms, wages and prices proved less easy to adjust downwards than in the nineteenth century. Therefore, output rather than prices declined as gold flowed out leading to reduced employment. Governments facing sharply rising unemployment in the early 1930s finally abandoned the gold standard.

In general, economists today rule out a return to the gold standard largely for reasons of practicality. Under completely fixed exchange rates, surpluses and deficits in the balance of payments can be corrected only by changes in relative prices in the countries concerned or, if prices are inflexible, by reducing or increasing real national income. For example, leaving aside the effect of capital flows, a country with a balance of payments deficit would need to deflate demand to the extent needed to reduce imports sufficiently to bring them into balance with export revenues. A country running a balance of payments surplus can continue to add to its foreign reserves, but a country with a deficit will sooner or later run out of reserves. The same could apply to countries suffering from large net capital outflows. For every deficit in the balance of payments of one country there must be an equal and offsetting surplus in the balance of payments of other countries. In principle, therefore, both deficit and surplus countries should act to correct payments imbalances. In practice, the burden of adjustment falls on the country running a balance of payments deficit to deflate its national income.

The Bretton Woods system
The second period of fixed exchange rates this century lasted from the end of the Second World War to the early 1970s. It emerged from a meeting of

the allied powers at a conference at Bretton Woods, New Hampshire in 1944, and hence is often referred to as the Bretton Woods System. Following the collapse of the gold standard in the 1930s, countries had attempted to gain competitive advantage by reducing their exchange rates, making exports relatively cheap and imports more expensive. Such action was primarily intended to boost employment prospects and was commonly referred to as a 'beggar my neighbour policy'. Ultimately, these measures damaged world trade.

At Bretton Woods it was agreed that fixed exchange rates should be restored but that a return to the gold standard was undesirable. A proposal advanced by the US delegation (the *White Plan*) formed the basis of the scheme finally endorsed. Under this scheme, all currencies were assigned a fixed exchange rate against the US dollar (a dollar parity), which in turn was assigned a fixed value against gold ($35 per troy ounce for official transaction purposes). As a consequence, cross exchange rates between currencies were fixed. The link between the US dollar and an officially recorded volume of gold acted as a break on the printing of surplus dollars by the US government and therefore maintained confidence in the US dollar.

The Bretton Woods system was not entirely a fixed exchange rate regime since currencies were permitted a small degree of flexibility ($\pm$ 1 per cent against the dollar parity until 1971). Large adjustments, however, could take place only where there were fundamental disequilibria in balance of payments (i.e. persistent and large deficits or surpluses) and only by agreement with other countries (though this latter condition was not always met). The system was supervised by an international body also established at Bretton Woods, namely the *International Monetary Fund* (IMF) based in Washington. Where countries suffered temporary balance of payments deficits, governments were expected to intervene in the foreign exchange markets to preserve the fixed parity using their foreign reserves. These reserves could be augmented by borrowing from the IMF up to agreed limits or from other central banks. At the same time, countries were expected to correct their balance of payments disequilibria by appropriate domestic fiscal and monetary policies – deficit countries deflating and surplus countries reflating. In practice, once again, the burden fell mainly on the deficit countries since the surplus countries lacked the same pressure to act.

In the case of the UK the sterling exchange rate was devalued only twice from 1945 to 1972. Once in 1949, when sterling was devalued from $4.03 to $2.80, and again in 1967 when the parity was reduced to $2.40. This contrasts vividly with experience under floating exchange rates which the UK adopted in June 1972. Since then the sterling exchange rate has fluctuated widely against the dollar and other currencies. The same is true for other leading currencies, which also abandoned fixed exchange rates in the early 1970s. Note that not all of sterling's fluctuation against the US dollar has been due to factors affecting the UK. Since the dollar floats up and down too, movements in the $/£ rate often occur because the dollar is changing in value on the international markets. This point should always be borne in mind when interpreting movements of one currency against another. It also explains why, in the media, sterling is sometimes quoted in terms of a basket of leading currencies or, more correctly, the *sterling exchange rate index*, which is a trade-weighted average of major currencies. Movements in this rate are more likely to reflect fundamental changes in the external value of sterling. Other currencies have similar trade-weighted measures.

The Bretton Woods system broke down for a number of reasons. Briefly, there was a growing lack of international liquidity; the main currencies held in central bank foreign reserves were the US dollar and, to a declining extent, especially after the 1967 devaluation, sterling. World reserves could finance 48 weeks' exports in 1948 but only 14 weeks' worth by the mid-1970s. This was exacerbated by declining confidence in the US dollar. To expand international liquidity, central banks had to be willing to hold dollars in their foreign reserves. There were no difficulties while confidence in the dollar was maintained. However, rising US government expenditures overseas (e.g. the Vietnam War) as well as the financing of America's space programme and the establishment of its social welfare system (the 'Great Society' programme) in the 1960s, led to a flood of dollars on to world markets and confidence sagged. In particular, dollars were traded for gold, which was considered to be a secure asset. At this time, however, gold had a fixed price under the Bretton Woods system of $35 per troy ounce, which the US government was committed to protect.

In 1968, following widespread conversion of dollar holdings into gold at the fixed rate by many countries, the US had to concede defeat and a two-price system for gold was introduced under which central banks continued to transfer gold among themselves at $35 per troy ounce, while gold was allowed to find its own value in the free market for non-official purposes. With a worsening US balance of payments on current account, however, this provided only a short respite. In August 1971, official dollar convertibility had to be suspended temporarily following renewed speculative activity. In December 1971 the Smithsonian Agreement officially devalued the dollar against other currencies and against gold (from $35 to $38 per troy ounce). Since other currencies were expressed in terms of the dollar, this meant that new currency parities were established (for sterling $2.67 = £1). This agreement was itself quickly overwhelmed, however, by world economic events. Rising inflation aggravated by a 300 per cent increase in world oil prices between 1972 and 1974, which undermined the balance of payments accounts of the leading industrial economies, meant that the Bretton Woods system finally collapsed.

Governments turned to floating their currencies, usually in the form of a *managed float*.

Managed exchange rates

A managed exchange rate system refers to a situation where exchange rates are determined in the main by the conditions of demand and supply, but central banks intervene from time to time to stabilize the rates or influence them in some way. Thus if sterling is depreciating rapidly the authorities could sell foreign currency reserves and buy sterling, helping to reduce the downward pressure. Similarly, to reduce an appreciating sterling value, the authorities could sell sterling and buy foreign currencies. In this way, intervention would help to smooth out the fluctuations in the exchange rate.

It should be appreciated that the degree to which the authorities are able to neutralize all fluctuations and hence keep the currency at a fixed rate, is limited. Central banks do not have sufficient reserves or lines of credit to intervene over a long period in foreign exchange markets, especially since around $1,200bn worth of currencies are traded each day in the world's foreign exchange markets. Consequently, a degree of flexibility in the exchange rate may have to be accepted. Managed flexibility can take a number of different forms such as *dirty floating* and *joint floating*.

In dirty floating, the decision as to when to intervene to support the currency and to what extent, is arbitrary. Some commentators argue that this describes the position taken by the UK authorities in the late 1980s when sterling came up against considerable downward pressure. The main objective, however, under dirty floating is to have reasonable stability in the exchange rate in order to maintain confidence in the currency – and perhaps in the government's general macroeconomic policy. The term dirty floating arises because governments attempt to 'manage' the float through foreign exchange intervention. An alternative, and less pejorative term, is a *managed float*.

Following the collapse of the Bretton Woods system of fixed exchange rates, a number of European countries set up a *joint float* in 1972 which became known as the *snake*. Under the snake, currencies were pegged to each other but were allowed a maximum variation between any two of the participating currencies of $\pm 2\frac{1}{4}$ per cent. They were then allowed to float freely (or within a band) against other currencies. At first the snake was a joint float against the US dollar though this link was broken in 1973 and it essentially evolved into a small 'club' of European currencies shadowing the deutschmark.

In 1979, the snake arrangement was replaced by the *European Monetary System* (EMS). This system has played a major role in the development of the Single European Market. Further details of the EMS are given in case study 3 in Chapter 10 but, briefly, the system is an extension of the snake. Until 1993, member currencies were managed so that they remained within margins of ±2¼ per cent (the Italian lira and later the Spanish peseta and sterling had a wider margin of ±6 per cent) against each other as well as against the *European Currency Unit* (ECU). This arrangement is known as the *Exchange Rate Mechanism* (ERM). The ECU is a *basket* unit of account whose value is derived as a weighted average of EMS member currencies, including sterling. It should be noted that the UK did not participate in the ERM arrangements from its inception because of fears that membership might prove unsustainable. The value of sterling was especially volatile in the late 1970s and early 1980s when the UK achieved petro-currency status following North Sea oil discoveries. The UK joined the ERM in October 1990. Two years later, however, a sterling crisis led the UK to abandon the system. A similar crisis led the lira also to leave the ERM while, a few months later, a run on the French franc caused the permissible margins of fluctuation to be widened from ±2¼ per cent to ±15 per cent. The events of 1992/3 illustrate the difficulty of maintaining fixed (or semi-fixed) exchange rates in a world of large capital flows in and out of countries. Again, we return to the central issues in this debate in Chapter 10.

Exchange rate systems compared

In this section we set out the central arguments both in favour of and against the adoption of fixed or floating exchange rates. Clearly, there is no simple answer as to which system is best: the choice will depend upon current economic conditions and, perhaps, the political philosophy ruling at a given point in time (free market versus intervention).

The case for floating exchange rates

The main attraction of adopting a floating exchange rate system is the apparent *automatic adjustment* to balance of payments problems. For example, if a country is experiencing inflationary problems which lead to a current account deficit, then depreciation of its currency should compensate for a loss of price competitiveness in international markets and pull the current account back towards equilibrium. Similarly, if a country is running a surplus on its current account, an appreciation in the exchange rate will raise the price of its exports and reduce the price of its imports moving the current account back to equilibrium.

Since floating exchange rates should automatically rectify a current account problem, there will be less need for a country to pursue demand management policies to reduce the demand for imports (i.e. to reduce imports through the absorption effect referred to in Chapter 8). The country will then be free to devote greater attention to solving internal problems (e.g. unemployment). At the same time, there will be less need for large reserves to be held by the authorities since the exchange rate does not have to be supported. All of these conclusions, however, only apply provided an appreciation or depreciation of the currency is not managed by the authorities but reflects demand and supply pressures in the foreign exchange markets. Also a floating system does not guarantee a current account balance because daily demand for and supply of leading currencies is affected by capital flows (including speculative activity relating to currency movements).

The case against floating exchange rates

Leaving aside the possibility that floating exchange rates may reflect movements of capital rather than trade flows (indeed capital movements may have a perverse effect on the balance of trade – see case study 5 in Chapter 10 which considers the US balance of payments), their main drawback lies in the uncertainty created in international trading and investment. This is particularly important for businesses. For example, if a British exporter invoices a foreign buyer in his own foreign currency, he will not be sure how much he will receive when this foreign currency is converted into domestic currency. However, such exchange rate uncertainty can be mitigated – at a price – by the use of *forward exchange contracts*, discussed later in this chapter (pages 170–2).

Floating exchange rates could also discourage some investors from investing overseas. This is more likely to be the case when exchange rates move erratically in large jumps leading to possible major capital losses – as well as potential capital gains, of course – when the investor realizes his investment or when interest, profits and dividends are remitted. The international investor faces exchange rate risk in addition to the usual risks attached to any investment activity. Again, the use of forward exchange contracts may mitigate this uncertainty.

The case for fixed exchange rates

Perhaps the strongest argument in favour of fixed exchange rates is that they impose some discipline on domestic monetary systems. For example, if a country's exports become uncompetitive and there is a persistent current account deficit, the authorities will have to resort to deflationary policies to improve the country's international payments position. Supply-side measures are also likely to be implemented, encouraging the restructuring of domestic industries. It has been suggested that the decline in sterling's value during the past twenty years provided little incentive for British industry to face up to the harsh reality of the need to restructure and invest in new plant and equipment. In other words, the depreciation of sterling simply extended product lifecycles and outmoded working practices but could not put off the inevitable. Moreover, insofar as a depreciating currency permits an exporter to pass on production costs, notably large wage settlements, a floating exchange rate system is not conducive to defeating domestic inflation. The UK Treasury's desire to hold sterling firm after 1986 owed much to the view that British industry should not be 'bailed out' by a sterling depreciation if it gave way to excessive wage demands (i.e. wage demands not paid for out of productivity gains).

The case against fixed exchange rates

As discussed earlier, fixed exchange rates may be maintained by the authorities by intervening in the foreign exchange markets, but this requires large amounts of foreign currency reserves. In practice, central banks have finite loan facilities and reserves (the Bank of England, for example, held foreign reserves to the value of $63.3bn in December 1994). At the same time, as the world's capital markets have expanded and opened up in recent years, the extent to which any one government is able to intervene to counteract the huge volumes of capital that now flow around the world is extremely limited. Even the seven leading countries known as the *Group of 7* or G7 (UK, Japan, USA, Canada, Italy, France and Germany) acting in concert have not always been able to forestall currency movements. Ultimately, as the saying goes, 'you cannot buck the market'. Therefore, irrevocably fixed exchange rates may be unrealistic today. The gold standard and the Bretton Woods system operated at a time when much smaller volumes of currency were traded daily and a much larger proportion of foreign exchange transactions were trade related. The Bretton Woods system collapsed because of widespread speculation against leading currencies, notably the US dollar.

There are two further arguments against fixed exchange rates. First, since the exchange rate is fixed any changes in international competitiveness cannot be reflected in currency movements. Therefore, the burden of adjustment to improve competitiveness must fall on the domestic economy through industrial restructuring, wage restraint and deflationary policies. Second, in attempting to keep the exchange rate fixed in the face of market forces the authorities lose control over the domestic money supply. This occurs because the money supply has to accommodate the fixed exchange rate. For example, in order to halt an appreciation in the value of the currency, the authorities might intervene by selling sterling in the foreign exchange markets. This sterling, however, will then tend to find its way back into the domestic economy thereby boosting the money supply. This in turn will add to inflationary pressures. Alternatively, interest rates might be reduced to stem capital inflows into the country but this will tend to encourage domestic credit expansion as people borrow more at the lower rates. Hence, the adoption of a fixed exchange rate system results in a loss of control over monetary policy – this is a major reason for the UK government's reluctance to take up full membership of the EMS by participating in the ERM before 1990 and why many economists oppose moves to link the European currencies together as a prelude to a single European currency.

The loss of UK monetary control in this context was graphically demonstrated in 1987 and 1988 when the then Chancellor of the Exchequer Nigel Lawson attempted to 'shadow the deutschmark' (at around DM 3 = £1). At the time market pressures were pushing sterling's value above this rate. Consequently, the authorities expanded the sterling money supply through foreign exchange intervention and by reducing UK interest rates and this contributed to a loss of control over the domestic money supply with, as witnessed in late 1988 and after, serious consequences for UK inflation.

Why does currency speculation occur?

We have referred to currency speculation in the foreign exchange markets on a number of occasions so far in this chapter. A simple example will help to underline why it can be very profitable and therefore why it occurs. Suppose that a speculator (an individual, a bank or a company with surplus funds) sold sterling to the sum of £100m on the foreign exchange market and bought US dollars, when the exchange rate was US$2 = £1. The speculator would receive US$200m. If this transaction reflected a general market tendency to sell sterling and buy dollars, the pound would *depreciate* against the dollar (or looking at it another way, the dollar would appreciate against the pound). Suppose the rate of exchange settled at US$1.80 = £1, the speculator could now repurchase £111m with the US$200m holding (i.e. $200m/$1.80). The profit on the transaction (ignoring costs such as trading commission and tax) is £11m.

Of course, if the speculator had judged the mood of the market incorrectly and sterling had *appreciated* against the dollar, instead of depreciating, then a loss would have resulted. Currency speculation carries inevitable risk unless the direction of change in the exchange rate can be predicted with complete certainty. Under the Bretton Woods system of fixed rates, the likelihood of a currency revaluation was low while a currency under selling pressure might well be devalued. Speculation, therefore, was often 'a one-way bet'. The same point applied to the European ERM, especially before the band was widened to ±15 per cent in August 1993. Under floating rates, however, currencies can just as easily go up in value as down. From this brief discussion, it should be obvious why governments deny that they would like to see the value of their currency fall in international markets, while not intervening extensively to prevent a fall (such as the UK in 1989). Any suggestion that a government harboured a desire to see its currency decline in value would trigger a bout of speculative selling because the future movement of the currency would be more predictable.

The determination of exchange rates

So far we have been analyzing different types of exchange rate system and the arguments for and against the adoption of each. A government, as a formal policy or on an *ad hoc* basis, may influence the value of its country's exchange rate relative to other currencies; also, the exchange rate is affected by the flow of exports and imports of goods, services and capital into and out of a country. However, there are a large number of other factors which interact within the economy to affect the external value of currencies and we now examine these.

At the macroeconomy level, changes in national income have an impact upon the demand for imports as well as goods and services produced for the domestic market which might otherwise be exported if demand for them did not exist in the home market. Changes in aggregate demand are therefore reflected in the demand for and supply of currencies on the foreign exchange markets and, hence, in exchange rates. At the same time, supply-side factors play an important role. The ability of an economy to increase output and employment eventually has implications for its balance of payments and ultimately its exchange rate.

Apart from the general state of the macroeconomy, both on the demand side and on the supply side, there are two further economic variables which have a direct impact upon exchange rates. These are:

1. The rate of domestic inflation relative to that in other countries.
2. Domestic interest rates compared with competing interest rates abroad.

The rate of inflation and the exchange rate

In general, differences in the rates of inflation between countries will be reflected in the exchange rates between their currencies. Countries experiencing higher rates of inflation will tend to experience depreciation in the external value of their currencies. The converse applies to countries experiencing lower rates of inflation than average; their exchange rates will tend to appreciate. These movements tend to occur gradually under freely floating exchange rates, but more slowly and falteringly where rates are managed or fixed because the authorities intervene to offset market movements, in ways already discussed.

Observations on the apparent inverse relationship between inflation rates and exchange rates led to the development of *purchasing power parity theory*. This attempts to explain changes in currency values exclusively in terms of relative rates of inflation in different countries. In essence, the theory predicts that the exchange rate of one currency against another currency will depend upon the *relative purchasing power* of these currencies in their own countries. For example, if £1 buys X amount of goods in the UK and $1.60 also buys the same X amount of goods in the USA, then the equilibrium exchange rate should be £1 = $1.60. If this is not the case, and ignoring transport and freight insurance costs, then goods will be imported from the cheaper country, creating a balance of trade deficit in the more expensive country, whose currency will tend to fall in value until the equilibrium rate is established. Thus, purchasing power parity theory states that an exchange rate varies according to relative price changes, so that:

$$\textit{Old} \text{ exchange rate} \times \frac{\text{Price level in country A}}{\text{Price level in country B}} = \textit{New} \text{ exchange rate}$$

The theory, however, has proved inadequate as an explanation of movements in exchange rates in the short term. In part this is because it ignores the importance of transport, insurance and other costs in assessing relative costs of goods. But also, relative costs and prices of non-traded goods included in the measurement of domestic inflation rates make comparison of these inflation rates unreliable in determining exchange rate equilibria, while capital flows can influence short-term exchange rate values. Nevertheless, purchasing power parity theory has been shown to have more validity in predicting the *long-term* movements of exchange rates. Countries that persistently experience relatively high inflation rates eventually also experience depreciation in the value of their currencies on the foreign exchange market under a floating exchange rate regime.

Interest rates and exchange rates

A strong link is also evident between interest rates and exchange rates. For example, high interest rates in one country relative to other countries will tend to attract inflows of capital from these lower interest-rate economies (unless there are other factors acting as a disincentive to invest, e.g.

political instability or a perception that the exchange rate of the country is about to fall). These capital flows will, in turn, raise the exchange rate of the recipient country. This relationship is particularly significant in the world's money and foreign currency markets today in equalizing interest rate differentials between the major international financial centres, as discussed in the following example which introduces the role of the *forward exchange market*.

Suppose that capital is allowed to flow unhindered between the USA and UK and that a three-month deposit of capital can earn a 14 per cent return in New York and a 10 per cent return in London. The 4 per cent margin between the returns will, everything else being equal, entice UK investors (speculators) to move sterling from London to New York, investing perhaps in short-term US dollar deposit accounts. This action requires them to *sell* sterling and *buy* dollars at the current (spot) exchange rate between the dollar and sterling. As a consequence, the supply of sterling will rise as the demand for the dollar rises, leading to an appreciation in the dollar's value and a fall in sterling's value on the foreign exchange market. It should be noted that it is not necessary in practice for funds to move from the UK to the USA. The City of London contains the world's largest Eurocurrency trading including the Eurodollar market. It is possible, therefore, to trade in US$ denominated amounts purely within the confines of the City.

It is possible that during the three-month deposit period, the value of the dollar could fall sharply (for whatever reason) against sterling. The consequent capital loss could then outweigh the greater return earned through the 4 per cent interest rate differential. To protect against this possibility, the UK investor could cover his liability by dealing in the *forward exchange market*. That is, he could buy dollars against the spot exchange rate for sterling, and simultaneously agree to sell dollars against sterling *three months forward*. This is known as a *forward contract*. The difference between the quoted spot and forward exchange rates is known as the *forward premium* (or *discount*) i.e. when the spot price of sterling rises above the forward price against the dollar, the pound is said to have a *forward discount* (when it falls below, a *forward premium*). It should be noted that the size of this premium or discount must exactly equal the difference between dollar and sterling interest rates (in this case 4 per cent) otherwise an opportunity will exist for *arbitrageurs* to make money by buying or selling in the spot or forward markets. It follows that forward exchange rates are determined by interest rate differentials rather than simply by market expectations of exchange rates in the future.

The example above also highlights the extent to which speculation in foreign exchange can itself be a stabilizing influence on exchange rate values. For example, if a country has a current account deficit on its balance of payments account then there will be downward pressure on its currency. If speculators take the view that such a deficit is only temporary, then they may be tempted to buy the currency when it is falling in value and sell again when its value rises as the current account returns to surplus later – hoping, of course, to make a profit in the process as detailed earlier in this chapter. In this way, any depreciation in the currency will be offset to some extent by the buying decisions of speculators.

In contrast, speculation may also be destabilizing, particularly where the volumes of currencies being bought and sold are so huge that they lead to changes in currency values that are not reflective of the underlying economic reality, i.e. exchange rates may *overshoot* or *undershoot* equilib-rium levels. On balance, many economists would argue that excessive speculation is destabilizing by creating uncertainty about currency values which, as we noted earlier, may damage international trading relationships and hence world trade and growth. On the other hand, this type of speculation is difficult to distinguish from sound commercial decisions by financiers, including corporate treasurers. If they believe a currency will shortly decline in value then it makes sense to sell the currency now. Recall, however, that the action of selling a currency, perhaps based upon a rumour in the markets that the currency is coming under pressure, has the effect of *causing* the value of the currency to fall.

Exchange rates and the balance of payments

On several occasions we have noted, generally, that floating exchange rates can correct a current account imbalance: the adjustment should be automatic via the market mechanism. Demand for a surplus country's currency will be rising, pushing up its exchange rate and thus making its exports more expensive and its imports cheaper. In this way a current account surplus will tend to be eliminated while the reverse process can be expected in the case of a deficit country.

In practice, this seemingly automatic mechanism does not always appear to work – or, if it does, it takes time for the effects to become evident. This situation is typical of that which has often faced the UK: despite a fall in the sterling exchange rate against nearly all other major currencies, the current account continues to be a problem. Why?

When currencies depreciate, it may take time for people to adjust their patterns of consumption and to change their investment plans. For example, British households and firms may continue to buy what they regard as high quality imports, despite the fact that a fall in sterling's value may have pushed up import prices. At the same time, foreigners may not respond immediately to the fall in sterling by placing immediate orders for UK goods – again, tastes and preferences take time to change. Thus, the initial responsiveness (i.e. elasticity) of demand for both imports and

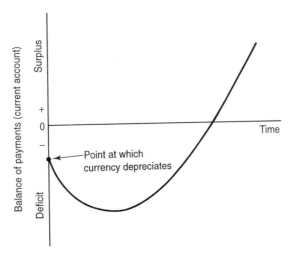

Figure 9.3 The J-curve effect.

exports as a consequence of changes in currency value may be quite low. Depreciation will lead to an improvement in the current account situation only if the sum of the price elasticities of demand for exports and for imports exceeds unity. This condition is popularly known as the *Marshall–Lerner condition*.[1]

If the Marshall–Lerner condition is not satisfied then, in fact, as the currency of a deficit country falls in value, the initial effect may be a *worsening* in the balance of payments. Also, given that the volumes of imports and exports are likely to remain unchanged in the short term, the total import bill (valued in domestic terms) will be rising faster than the total revenue from exports (valued in domestic terms) as the currency depreciates. Indeed, if exports are originally priced in sterling, then with demand unchanged the sterling revenue will stay the same. Hence the current account can deteriorate initially, as illustrated in Figure 9.3.

However, as Figure 9.3 also suggests, in time the balance of payments position is likely to improve as demand for the now cheaper-priced exports expands (assuming that the foreign price of the exported goods is reduced to reflect the depreciation) and as demand for the now more expensive imports falls. In other words, depreciation eventually leads to an improvement in the current account, giving rise to the *J-curve effect* as shown in the figure. Economists have estimated that it may take on average eighteen months for the UK balance of payments to start to improve following a depreciation in sterling.

Of course, the opposite logic applies in the case of surplus countries facing an appreciation in their currencies. In the short term, if demand is

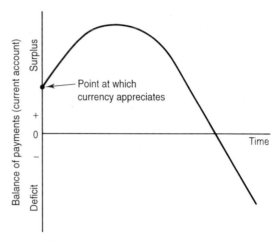

Figure 9.4 Inverted J-curve effect.

sluggish to respond to relative price changes, appreciation is likely to boost the current account surplus further. Eventually, however, it is to be expected that the volume of imports and exports will respond to the price changes as shown in Figure 9.4. This is known as the *inverted J-curve effect*.

As noted earlier, despite a general fall in sterling's external value against a number of leading currencies, the UK's trade performance sometimes deteriorated. This suggests that factors other than relative prices are important in determining the extent to which a current account deficit can be reversed. Indeed, some economists argue that price considerations are often given too prominent a place in explanations of trade flows. They stress a number of other reasons for the weakness in Britain's balance of payments position. It is argued, for example, that UK manufacturers have failed to move up-market over the last two decades in terms of quality, design and marketing, restricting the growth in exports and encouraging import penetration. In other words, it is stressed that *non-price* factors have been dominant, reflecting the slow pace of structural change and supply-side inflexibility in British industry. It is also the case that when sterling has depreciated exporters have often chosen to retain exporting prices and improve their profit margins, thus forestalling the improvement in price competitiveness that depreciation implies.

Exchange rates and business

Erratic changes in exchange rates can, as noted earlier, increase the uncertainty facing management in its decision making. Given the likelihood of a lengthy time period between winning an export order or placing an import order and the final delivery of the goods and the settling of accounts, exchange rate fluctuations can make all the difference between a profit or a loss on the transaction. In this way, floating exchange rates may discourage trade and investment decisions though, as discussed above, short-term risks can be overcome by the use of forward exchange markets, where firms can agree to buy currency at a given future date at a contracted price. This will, however, involve transaction costs such as commission. Forward contracts cannot usually be negotiated for more than a year in advance, so they cannot be used to cover longer-term risks in international trade and investment. Other methods to reduce exchange rate risk include:

1. Use of *forecasts* of exchange rate movements.
2. *Risk-spreading* through having a range of overseas suppliers and export markets trading in different currencies, in the hope that this will provide some security.
3. *Hedging*, which is useful where there is no forward market; a corporate treasurer can deal in foreign currencies and deposit sums in different currencies as a hedge against currency fluctuations.
4. *Investing in foreign subsidiaries:* multinational companies reduce exchange rate risk by sourcing and supplying in various countries; exchange rate movements may also lead them to reallocate work between national plants to retain competitiveness and to protect profits.

Fluctuations in exchange rates require managers to make difficult economic decisions. This is illustrated by the following example. Suppose a UK firm is exporting a luxury car selling at £20,000 in the UK and, at an exchange rate of $1.75 = £1, $35,000 in the USA (ignoring freight and insurance charges, etc.). If the company currently sells 1,000 vehicles per annum in the USA, its total earnings there are $35m. Now suppose that the exchange rate appreciates to US$2 = £1, the UK manufacturer faces two choices:

- To continue to sell in the USA at the existing price of $35,000 but now receive only £17,500 as against £20,000 per vehicle in sterling ($35,000 ÷ $2). Hence total receipts fall by £2.5m (£17.5m as against £20m).
- To raise the US price to compensate for the sterling appreciation. The price of vehicles in the USA would therefore rise to $40,000. But at the higher price fewer cars are likely to be sold.

Which of the two options will be chosen may depend upon the *price sensitivity of demand* (or *elasticity*) for the vehicles in the USA. If they are price sensitive then raising the price to $40,000 might lead to *lower* sales receipts in sterling than if the price had been left unchanged. For example, if vehicle sales fell to 750 per annum, total revenue in sterling would be £15m (750 × $40,000 ÷ $2). A similar managerial decision would have to be faced if the currency *depreciated*: in this case whether to reduce the overseas sales price by an equivalent amount or whether to sell at the same price but with a healthier profit margin in sterling terms. Again, the price sensitivity of exports will be an important deciding factor. Also relevant are expectations as to how long the depreciation will last (there is no point in reducing prices today and then increasing them again next week), and whether the firm has sufficient capacity to produce more output for export (there is no point in stimulating export sales through price reductions which cannot be met).

Concluding remarks

Fluctuating exchange rates affect production costs if imported raw materials and components are required. At the same time, downward pressure on the currency may lead to higher domestic inflation which is likely to feed through into higher wage demands, with implications for employment, profits and investment plans.

Movements in exchange rates add a further and unwelcome element of risk and uncertainty in business decision making today. For this reason many people in business demand greater exchange rate stability. But stable exchange rates (within or outside a mechanism such as the ERM) have pitfalls as well as advantages. Without exchange rate flexibility, cost and price increases in excess of those experienced in competitor countries must eventually lead to a decline in exports and a rise in imports. The consequent deterioration in the current account will lead government to introduce economic measures designed to deflate demand and thus reduce economic growth to bring down inflation. This is likely to feed through into lower profitability, plant closures and unemployment.

At the same time, however, floating exchange rates may not be the answer. Floating rates may be inflationary, in the sense that they enable governments to postpone remedial action to reduce inflationary pressures, while depreciation increases the prices of imported goods which adds to inflation. For this reason some economists have argued for the UK's re-entry into the EMS Exchange Rate Mechanism. Once sterling's rate against the other member currencies is fixed again then the UK authorities, to maintain the rate, must bring the country's inflation rate close to that of the other members, and notably that of Germany which has a history of 'sound money'.

Note

1. In its simplest form the Marshall–Lerner condition states that the (absolute) values of the price elasticities of demand for exports and imports must sum to more than unity if a fall in the external value of the currency is to lead to an improvement in the current account of the balance of payments. This follows because the volume of exports increases and the volume of imports decreases as export prices fall (denominated in foreign currency) and import prices increase (denominated in domestic currency) when the exchange rate falls. *Elasticity* is simply a numerical measure of the responsiveness of demand with respect to these price changes. If the (absolute) price elasticity of demand for exports plus the (absolute) price elasticity of demand for imports exceeds unity, then the increased cost of imports (in terms of the domestic currency) is outweighed by the value of the growth in exports. Hence the current account of the balance of payments improves.

10

Case studies

These case studies are intended to test the reader's understanding and awareness of the concepts and principles covered in this book. They cover a wide range of topics dealing with both domestic and international economic issues and end with a series of questions for individual consideration or class discussion. Intentionally, we have not included specimen answers: first, because the complexity of the economy is such that there is no such thing as an absolutely right way of managing the economy, and second, because we do not want to pre-empt class discussion where the book is being used on business and management courses.

The cases deal with the following aspects of the macroeconomy:

1. Determination of economic activity.
2. The relationship between inflation and unemployment.
3. Prospects for European Economic and Monetary Union.
4. The international debt crisis.
5. Analysis of the US twin deficits.
6. Linkages between money, growth, prices and interest rates.
7. Outlook for the economy.

Other cases may be found in some of the books listed on pages 208–9 as further reading.

1 Determination of economic activity

We saw in Chapter 4 that expenditure is an important determinant of economic activity. Based on the expenditure method, GDP may be broken

Table 10.1 Shifts in GDP composition (1979–89).

	Change (% of GDP)			
	Consumption expenditure (C)	Gross capital formation (I)	General government consumption (G)	Net exports (X–M)
USA	+3.6	−3.8	+0.9	−0.7
Japan	−2.1	+0.3	−0.5	+2.3
Germany	−2.3	−1.4	−1.0	+4.7
France	+1.8	−1.8	+0.6	−0.6
UK	+3.5	+0.9	−0.3	−4.1
Italy	+1.8	−2.8	+2.3	−1.3
Total OECD[a]	+1.6	−2.1	+0.4	+0.1

[a] 25 major economies including those above.
Note: figures have been rounded so as to add to zero for all countries.
Source: OECD, *National Accounts* (various years).

down into the following components: consumption expenditure (C), investment expenditure (I), government expenditure (G) and exports (X) net of imports (M). Thus the composition of gross domestic product (GDP) is:

$$C + I + G + (X - M)$$

Table 10.1 shows shifts in the composition of GDP for certain major OECD economies over the period 1979–89.

Questions

1. Discuss the relative contribution to GDP by each of the components for each country and the OECD as a whole during the period 1979–89.
2. What have been the implications of such shifts in GDP composition for each country in terms of:
   • government finances?
   • exchange rates?
   • balance of payments (current and capital account flows)?
3. Assess the consequences of these relative shifts for the global economy in the future.

2 The relationship between inflation and unemployment

In an article published in 1958, A.W. Phillips indicated on the basis of UK data for the period 1861–1957 that there was a strong negative relationship

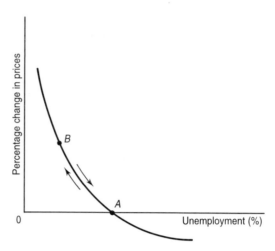

Figure 10.1 The Phillips curve.

between the rate of change of money wages and the level of unemployment. The statistical analysis indicated that the relationship had been markedly stable for a continuous period of almost a hundred years with a higher unemployment rate being associated with a lower rate of growth of money wage rates. Soon after the original research was completed, it was also argued that there was also a significant and stable negative relationship between the rate of change of prices (i.e. inflation) and the level of unemployment. This is not really surprising since wage increases not paid for out of higher productivity are likely to be passed on to consumers in the form of price increases. Hence the correlation between wage and price inflation is likely to be statistically high. This relationship between the growth of prices on the one hand and unemployment on the other has become known as the *Phillips curve* (see Figure 10.1).

The work of Phillips seemed to offer government a range of policy choices. It suggested that governments could trade-off a particular level of unemployment against a particular rate of inflation. For example, if aggregate demand were stimulated (say, via tax cuts and/or an expansion of government spending), this could reduce unemployment but at the expense of a higher rate of inflation and vice versa. In other words, governments could fine-tune aggregate demand and push the economy up and down the Phillips curve (say from A to B and then back to A again). Furthermore, it was suggested that unemployment could not be reduced below its natural rate shown as point A in Figure 10.1, without triggering inflationary pressures. As we saw in Chapter 7, this natural rate is associated with equilibrium in the labour market where the demand for labour at a given real wage rate is equal to the supply of labour – any

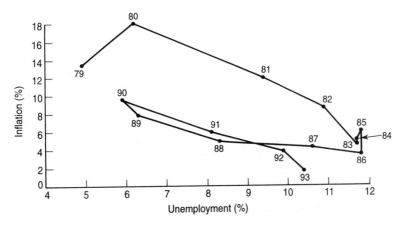

Figure 10.2 UK inflation and unemployment 1979–93 (*Source: Economic Trends Annual Supplement 1994*).

unemployment remaining is 'natural' in the sense that either those out of work do not want to work at the going wage rate or their services are no longer in demand (because of structural changes in the economy; this is referred to as *structural* unemployment). Some workers will also be temporarily out of work due to the fact that the transition from one job to another may not be instantaneous (referred to as *frictional* unemployment), or because of seasonal factors.

For much of the 1960s many governments actively attempted to manage their economies on the basis of the Phillips curve relationship. It provided an attractive policy choice which could be triggered at suitable times (perhaps reducing unemployment in the run-up to elections). However, towards the end of the 1960s the relationship began to look unstable as unemployment, wages and prices all began to rise together. Figure 10.2 plots the rate of retail price inflation against the unemployment rate for the UK for the period 1979 to 1993. During the late 1970s and early 1980s there was, in fact, a marked outward shift in the relationship with stagflation being a prominent feature of the economy (rising unemployment associated with growing inflation). However, as shown in the diagram, the relationship seemed to shift back towards the origin after the mid-1980s.

With the stability of a trade-off coming into question, monetarist economists mounted a successful assault upon the Phillips curve. They argued that lower unemployment could be achieved only by accepting an ever rising rate of inflation. Thus the relationship between inflation and unemployment was not stable as the Phillips curve implied. Monetarists maintained that Keynesian demand expansion initially raises prices and thereby lowers real wages (wages adjusted for prices). This increases the

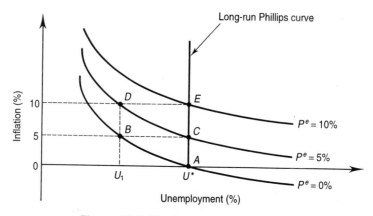

Figure 10.3 The long-run Phillips curve.

demand for labour. Unemployment falls but soon employees bargain for money wage increases to offset the fall in real wages experienced. The resulting increase restores real wages but threatens to cause a return of unemployment as employers shed labour. If the government reacts in a Keynesian fashion and stokes up demand to prevent this, prices rise again and real wages fall until such time as workers successfully press for a restoration of income. As each of these price–wage cycles leads to a higher level of real prices, Keynesian techniques prove inflationary.

This approach to the Phillips curve is illustrated in Figure 10.3. In the diagram, U^* is the 'natural rate of unemployment', where the level of inflation is fully anticipated and real wages are determined by demand and supply conditions in the labour market. For simplicity assume no productivity growth and that the economy is currently at point A on the unemployment axis experiencing zero inflation. This is the rate of inflation which people expect to continue; in other words inflationary expectations (P^e) are zero.

Suppose now that the government is dissatisfied with this level of unemployment and decides to increase aggregate demand in an attempt to reduce unemployment from U^* to U_1. Inflation rises, in Figure 10.3, say to 5 per cent. Wages are contractual and generally do not respond immediately. More labour is employed at the lower real wage and unemployment falls to point B along the Phillips curve, $P^e = 0\%$. In time, however, workers will demand higher wages to restore real purchasing power. What happens now depends critically on how expectations of inflation adjust. Let us assume that the expected rate of inflation is the present rate of 5 per cent and therefore wage demands are 5 per cent. As real wages return to their initial level, firms will release labour and unemployment will return to the level U^* – but this will now be associated with a rate of inflation of 5 per cent. Thus, the economy has now moved from B to C, and not from B back to A, in Figure 10.3.

Suppose the government now increases aggregate demand again in an attempt to lower unemployment from U^* to U_1. Once more prices rise, say from an inflation rate of 5 per cent to 10 per cent. Real wages fall but this time causing a movement along the new Phillips curve associated with inflationary expectations of 5 per cent (i.e. $P^e = 5\%$), from point C to D. Workers respond with a corresponding 10 per cent wage demand which restores real wages and there is a movement from point D to E. Unemployment rises back to U^* but it is now associated with an inflation rate of 10 per cent. In other words, every round of increase in aggregate demand leads to a temporary fall in unemployment but a ratcheting up of the inflation rate and inflationary expectations. The economy returns to a rate of unemployment U^* but at an increasingly higher inflation rate. This gives rise to the so-called 'long-run Phillips curve'. Thus, for Professor Friedman and his followers, however much the rate of inflation is increased, unemployment will have a natural tendency to return to U^*. There is only the possibility of a *short-run* trade-off between unemployment and inflation. It follows that in the *long run* there is no trade-off. Thus the level of unemployment represented by U^* has become known as the *natural rate of unemployment* (NRU) or the *non-accelerating-inflation rate of unemployment* (NAIRU). The way to reduce unemployment permanently is to reduce the 'natural rate' through supply-side reforms that make the labour market more flexible (see Chapter 7).

The careful reader will have noted that the above mechanism depended upon how inflation expectations changed. In the example, a simple approach was adopted in which workers always responded to the previous price rise. But in practice it is likely that workers would quickly learn that inflation was rising and would react by demanding wages that compensated for both past inflation and expected inflation, in which case unemployment might not fall much when aggregate demand was increased, even for a short period. Indeed, the extreme case would be one in which when government decided to raise aggregate demand workers correctly recognized the inflationary consequences and immediately obtained offsetting wage increases. In this case, real wages would not fall and therefore nor would unemployment.

In practice, it seems that unemployment can be reduced for a short time by Keynesian policies but the latter point emphasizes the critical importance of inflation expectations in determining policy outcomes. So-called 'rational expectations theory' suggests that workers quickly appreciate that their earlier inflation forecasts were wrong and adjust their inflation predictions and behaviour accordingly. They quickly learn to base wage demands not just on past inflation but on all information available to them regarding future inflation. Workers do not persistently underestimate the inflation rate.

Questions

1. What explanations can you give for the apparent collapse of the Phillips curve:

   (a) during the 1970s?

   (b) during the early 1980s?

2. What evidence is there to suggest that a trade-off between unemployment and inflation is likely to re-emerge in the 1990s and beyond in the UK?

3 Prospects for European Economic and Monetary Union

Background

A desire to create an environment of exchange rate stability and close economic co-operation has been a consistent goal of the member countries of the European Union (EU), and its various forerunner unions, since the 1950s. Full Economic and Monetary Union (EMU) would represent the ultimate culmination of the various arrangements and agreements (not all of which have survived) that have been in operation since then. Particularly relevant among these in the process towards EMU have been the European Monetary System (EMS), the Exchange Rate Mechanism (ERM) and the European Currency Unit (ECU).

The Delors Committee of Central Bankers, charged in 1988 to outline and prepare the various steps leading to EMU, defined monetary union in terms of the following:

- the total and irreversible convertibility of currencies;
- complete liberalization of capital transactions;
- full integration of banking and financial markets;
- the elimination of fluctuation margins and the irrevocable locking of exchange rate parities.

Economic union is therefore envisaged as involving a single market (within which goods, services, people and capital are able to move freely), greater competition policy and other measures aimed at strengthening market mechanisms and greater macroeconomic policy co-ordination. While it was further argued that the adoption of a single currency is not strictly necessary for the creation of EMU, the Delors Report suggested that by demonstrating the irreversibility of the move to EMU, it would be desirable.

Advantages and disadvantages of EMU

The arguments in favour of EMU may be summed up as follows:

1. greater efficiency gains and greater transparency in terms of the competitiveness of member countries;
2. savings on foreign exchange transactions costs for businesses and individuals;
3. the elimination of exchange rate uncertainty;
4. reductions in interest rates (which previously embodied an exchange risk premium);
5. a stimulus to investment and growth;
6. greater trade and capital movements, particularly by smaller companies, due to the reduction in risk induced by exchange rate movements;
7. improved prospects for greater price stability.

However, opponents of EMU have stressed the dangers of moving towards greater unity. Their arguments may be summed up as follows:

1. erosion of national sovereignty by participating states;
2. the loss of the exchange rate as an instrument of economic adjustment at the national level;
3. the transfer of national monetary policy to a single authority (the European Central Bank, ECB) which will be operationally independent;
4. fiscal discipline by member states to support the EU's general economic policies;
5. potentially higher taxes in the stronger economies to support structural adjustment in the weaker states;
6. inappropriate interest rate movements for certain economies.

Implementing EMU

The EMU process was outlined by the Delors Report in 1989, with the actual timetable formulated in the Maastricht Treaty of December 1991. There are three distinct phases.

Stage 1
This began on 1 July 1990, and included complete liberalization of capital movements within the EU countries as well as the completion of the

internal market programme resulting from the European Single Market which came into being on 1 January 1993. This stage also envisaged greater economic convergence, including the tighter co-ordination of monetary, fiscal and economic policy and a doubling of structural fund resources as a means to help economic imbalances. A further aim (not yet realized) was the inclusion of all EU currencies within the narrow ± 2.25 per cent band of the ERM, and a strengthening of the role of the Committee of Central Bank Governors as a forerunner to the creation of the European Central Bank. In the institutional field, it was necessary to prepare and ratify the changes to the Treaty of Rome required for the start of Stage 2. This was achieved by the Maastricht Treaty.

Stage 2
This began on 1 January 1994 with the establishment of the European Monetary Institute (EMI) as the forerunner of the European Central Bank which will start operation in Stage 3. The EMI is to lay the technical and logistical groundwork for the ECB, including the formulation of a common monetary policy. The extent of its influence, however, in European monetary affairs is still limited as ultimate responsibility for monetary policy decisions during Stage 2 is to remain with the national authorities. Nevertheless, policy co-ordination among participating countries is a vital element of Stage 2. In this context the EMI will monitor and analyze EU members' fiscal and monetary policies, and make recommendations. During Stage 2, all central banks are expected to be granted independence, so as to ensure the autonomy of the ECB.

Stage 3
The final stage of EMU will start with a move to permanently fixed exchange rates, leading to a single currency. This will be coupled with the adoption of a single monetary policy. Responsibility for the formulation and the implementation of the latter would be transferred in full to the ECB. A single currency is planned eventually to replace national currencies completely. During Stage 3, participating countries would be expected to support the EU's general economic policies, including fiscal discipline, and this would be subject to monitoring by the EU Commission and the Council of Ministers.

EMU qualifying criteria

The specific timing of the move from Stage 2 to Stage 3 of EMU allows limited scope for manoeuvre. Five conversion criteria have been set in order for countries to qualify for membership of EMU. The conversion criteria are as follows:

- *Price stability*: a rate of inflation no more than 1.5 per cent above the average rate of the three best-performing member states during the previous year.
- *Public finances* (two criteria): (1) the annual general government deficit should not exceed 3 per cent of GDP; and (2) the general government debt ratio should not exceed 60 per cent of GDP.
- *Exchange rate stability*: a country's currency must have remained within the normal fluctuation bands of the ERM for at least two years, without devaluing on its own initiative against any other member currency.
- *Long-term interest rates*: during the previous year, average long-term interest rates must not have been more than 2 percentage points above the comparable rates of the countries with the lowest inflation.

Questions

1. Is the goal of EMU either attainable or desirable?
2. Assess the UK's position regarding membership of EMU.
3. What particular challenges is the UK likely to face if it accepts a single currency?
4. What particular benefits will the UK obtain from full participation in EMU?
5. How might the development of the Single European Market and Economic and Monetary Union within Europe be viewed from an *external* perspective
6. Which countries within the EU are unlikely to be eligible for membership of EMU in the near future? Why?
7. How will a widening of membership of the European Union affect progress towards EMU?

4 The international debt crisis

Following a 300 per cent increase in world oil prices between 1972 and 1974, the oil exporting countries of the Middle East were left with large current account surpluses in their balance of payments. To offset this, they were encouraged by Western governments and banks to invest their surpluses in the world capital markets. The Western banks acted as financial intermediaries, recycling these funds to borrowing countries. Chief among the borrowers were the 'middle income', less developed countries (LDCs), notably Argentina, Venezuela, Brazil and Mexico. These countries were benefiting at the time from buoyant world prices for their commodities, notably raw materials, and had an apparently insatiable demand for external funds for private investment and government spending. By 1982, when the debt crisis broke, the total indebtedness of non-oil-exporting LDCs stood at US$814.4bn.

The onset of world recession in 1979, however, led to a fall in the prices of most raw materials. Oil exporting debtor nations, such as Venezuela and Mexico, benefited from a further rise in oil prices in 1979–80, but faced special problems from 1986 when the price of oil fell from over US$27.80 a barrel in 1985 to around US$13. Economic difficulties were compounded by higher interest rates on debt resulting from tight monetary policies pursued in the industrialized countries to bring down their inflation rates. Major debtor nations experienced an appreciation in real interest rates of 45 per cent between 1979 and 1982. In turn, higher interest rates in the USA led to an appreciation in the value of the US dollar in which most of the international debts were denominated, aggravating even further the problems facing debtor nations.

Faced with a deteriorating economic situation in the debtor countries, the inflow of new capital into these countries declined sharply from 1982 onwards. The resulting flight of capital added to the foreign exchange burden of funding interest payments. Since 1984, instead of capital flowing from the industrialized countries to the LDCs, there was actually a net outflow of funds from the LDCs to the industrial countries. In August 1982 the debt crisis broke when Mexico called a moratorium on its debt repayments, triggering similar action in a number of other debtor countries. Since debts have to be serviced out of foreign exchange, one useful measure of the debt burden is interest payments as a ratio of export earnings. Normally, a ratio of over 20 per cent is considered difficult to service without imposing serious strain upon an economy. In 1986 the fifteen most heavily indebted LDCs operated with ratios averaging over 43 per cent. Consequently, these countries had to deflate domestic demand so as to switch from running trade deficits to registering trade surpluses and their economic growth rates stagnated (see Table 10.2).

The economic implications of the international debt crisis have extended beyond the debtor countries and their exporters to the Western banking system. In 1984 the nine largest US banks had outstanding LDC debts equivalent to 263 per cent of their capital. Initially, the banks attempted simply to reschedule the debts, but later the banks had to accept that many of the debts would never be repaid. By early 1989, West German banks had made bad debt provisions in the order of 50 per cent of their LDC debts; French banks 45 per cent; Canadian banks 35 per cent; and US banks 30 per cent. This was not achieved without pain. For example, because of these bad debt provisions the Midland Bank in 1988 became the first UK

Table 10.2 Economic performance of LDCs.

	1973–9 (average) %	1983–8 (average) %
All LDCs		
Percentage export volume growth	2.6	4.7
Percentage import volume growth	8.5	−3.1
Fifteen most heavily indebted LDCs		
Percentage real growth in GDP	5.9	1.9

Source: International Monetary Fund.

Table 10.3 Capital flows to Latin America.

Changes between 1984–89 and 1990–93, as % of GDP	Capital inflow	Investment
Argentina	4.7	−3.0
Bolivia	2.9	3.4
Chile	8.9	3.7
Ecuador	3.5	0.0
Mexico	6.5	3.8
Peru	7.2	2.9
Uruguay	2.2	1.9
Venezuela	2.7	−4.0
Average	4.5	0.9

Source: *Latin American Capital Flows: Living with Volatility*, a Study Group Report for the Group of Thirty, 1994; *Lloyds Bank Economic Bulletin*, No 1 February 1995.

clearing bank since the war to record a loss in its annual accounts. Manufacturers Hanover, the US bank with the largest exposure to LDC debts, would have had only around one-third of its equity left if it had marked down all of its Latin American loans to their current market value in 1989.

Since 1989, the threat to the world economy from international indebtedness has receded (temporarily?) and confidence within the banking sector has been restored. Table 10.3 shows that a number of countries, notably Argentina, Brazil and Venezuela, have experienced large capital inflows relative to their GDPs during the early 1990s. Recession in Europe and North America has increased the attractiveness of these markets for international investors. Interestingly, however, as also shown in Table 10.3, these capital inflows may have had little impact on domestic investment (except insofar as the domestic investment level might have been even lower without them).

Capital inflows should help finance domestic investment but they have costs in terms of the initial tendency for trade deficits to widen as imports of consumption and capital goods rise. Capital inflows may also put upward pressure on exchange rates, further widening trade deficits and leading to domestic economic upheaval.

A new Mexican currency crisis in January 1995, when there was a widespread loss of international confidence in the Mexican peso, illustrates once again the volatility of world capital flows. Although the international banking system is today probably more capable of weathering a spate of major debt defaults than it was in the early to mid-1980s, such an event would still cut a swathe through bank balance sheets. Renewed major Latin American defaults on international debt (perhaps now compounded by defaults by the new governments of heavily indebted central and eastern Europe) could still trigger a major crisis in the international economy.

Questions

1. What effect would a renewed international debt crisis have on the world economy?

2. What macroeconomic solutions might be considered by national governments to alleviate the economic effects if such a crisis arose?

3. What lessons are there for companies operating internationally as a result of the growth of international capital flows?

5 Analysis of the US twin deficits

Since 1980 the USA, the world's largest economy, has become the world's largest debtor. Large budget deficits under President Reagan and later under the Bush and Clinton administrations resulted in a more than trebling of the US national debt. The rise in the budget deficit in the early 1980s and its continuation into the 1990s and beyond on current policies, is detailed in Figure 10.4. An underlying structural deficit (government spending exceeding taxation) was compounded in the early 1980s by a cyclical deficit reflecting a downturn in the US economy (more government spending and a lower than expected growth in tax revenues). Later, as the economy recovered, increases in government spending, notably defence as well as tax cuts in 1982 which were introduced to stimulate the supply-

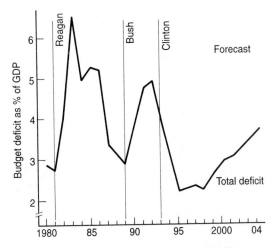

Figure 10.4 US budget deficits. *Source*: US Congressional Budget Office.

side of the economy, served to keep the overall budget deficit at historically high levels. The effect of the economic recession on government finances after 1989 is clearly visible.

Worries in Congress eventually led in 1985 to the passing of the Gramm–Rudman–Hollings Act which established budget deficit targets for each fiscal year. This legislation, however, soon fell by the wayside. The 1990 Budget Enforcement Act, which capped all government discretionary spending and restricted the budgetary impact of spending on entitlements (e.g. pensions) was more successful, but still left a budget deficit of around 5 per cent of GDP by 1993.

During the 1980s high interest rates were one important result of the large budget deficits, as the US administration resorted to tapping world savings. This tended to push up interest rates in other countries competing for international capital. As international investors scrambled to buy dollars to invest in US Treasury securities, this drove up the value of the US dollar on the foreign exchanges. Consequently, US exports were made less competitive and imports more competitive, resulting in a large and persistent US current account deficit on the balance of payments. As a percentage of GDP, the US current account went from a surplus of 0.2 per cent in 1981 to a peak deficit of 3.2 per cent in 1986, before falling back to between 2 and 3 per cent in the late 1980s. The appreciation of the US dollar was reversed after 1985 when the US central bank, the Federal Reserve, brought the value of the US dollar down by increasing the money supply and reducing interest rates. Particularly in terms of the strong Japanese yen, the US dollar has depreciated sharply since 1985 falling to below 100 yen to the dollar in late 1994 and early 1995 (Figure 10.5).

Figure 10.5 The depreciating dollar.

The budget deficit is often perceived to be the cause of the large balance of payments deficit on current account. Some economists have even suggested that the US balance of payments deficit cannot be eliminated until the government's budget is balanced. We can better appreciate this argument if we use and develop some of the basic national income accounting introduced in Chapter 3. The national product or output (NP) is made up of goods bought by consumers (C), government (G), firms for investment (I) and foreigners in the form of exports (X), i.e.:

$$NP = C + I + G + X$$

Similarly, the national income is spent, giving rise to national expenditure (NE), on domestically produced consumer goods and services (C) or saved (S) or it can be taken in tax (T) or spent on imports (M), i.e.:

$$NE = C + S + T + M$$

(In both of the above equations C is expressed net of expenditure taxes and subsidies.) Since NE must equal NP by definition (see Chapter 3) and since C is common to both of the above equations, it follows that:

$$I + G + X = S + T + M$$

Rearranging into sectors of the economy – international trade $(X$ and $M)$, the capital market $(S$ and $I)$, and the government sector $(G$ and $T)$ – we can express this last equation in the form:

$$(X - M) = (S - I) + (T - G)$$

From this we can see that if the government increases its budget deficit ($T - G$) and the difference between private saving and investment ($S - I$) stays constant, then any gap between total domestic leakages from the circular flow of income ($S + T$) and total domestic injections into the circular flow ($I + G$) must rise (for an explanation of injections and leakages see Chapter 4) and so, therefore, must the current account deficit ($X - M$) i.e. M will exceed X as imports are sucked into the economy. This result, whereby a current account deficit arises from an increase in domestic aggregate demand (as the consequence of, say, a budget deficit), arises from the *absorption effect*, i.e. imports are 'absorbed' into the economy. Everything else being equal, to rectify the current account deficit the gap between T and G can be reduced either by raising taxes or by cutting public spending (or both). Alternatively, by holding spending at around current levels, if national income is rising, *fiscal drag* (see Chapter 5) will lead to higher tax receipts and this in time will reduce the budget deficit significantly. This approach to cutting the deficit avoids some hard political choices and not surprisingly has been the preferred option of the Bush and Clinton administrations.

The idea that cutting the budget deficit will improve the US balance of payments position depends crucially, however, upon the gap between I and S staying unchanged. In the 1980s, all major economies experienced a decline in household savings – in the case of the USA from around 8 per cent of disposable income in 1980 to a low of 3 per cent in 1987. Should private sector, including non-personal (i.e. corporate), savings fall and private investment rise or stay constant then the gap between I and S will increase, in turn worsening the balance of payments position. Indeed, it should be appreciated from the sector equation above that if investment expenditure exceeds savings then a current account balance (where expenditure on exports equals expenditure on imports) *requires* the government to run a budget *surplus* equal to the difference between I and S.

The US budget deficit has worsened the country's balance of payments position. Recently, legislation was introduced into Congress aimed at forcing the president to balance the budget. But from the above discussion it should be obvious that balancing the budget does not guarantee that balance of payments problems will disappear. Also, we might ask what would be the ramifications for the UK and other leading trading nations if the USA removed its deficit? The USA still accounts for a large share of OECD output and is, for example, the UK's and Japan's largest single market. Therefore, a decline in economic activity in the USA is likely to have a profound impact upon other countries. Cutting government spending sharply, everything else being equal, would be deflationary. One result would be a fall in demand for imports in the USA. Another might be a fall in the value of the US dollar and hence an increase in the competitiveness of US exports in world markets. This could occur if the administration attempted to minimize the overall deflationary effects of the budget reduction by loosening monetary policy and bringing down interest rates. The extent to which such events would affect other economies and firms outside the USA depends, of course, upon the wider impact of these changes upon the world economy. Would, for example, interest rates fall worldwide in response to a cut in the USA? What is clear is that firms exporting to the USA have profited recently because of a buoyant US demand. A major deflation in the USA to correct the twin deficits could throw all of this into reverse.

Questions

1. What measures could the US government take to correct the budget deficit? Consider the demand-side and supply-side effects of your recommendations.
2. Consider more fully the likely impact of reducing the US budget deficit on the US economy and the world economy.
3. What are the implications of a depreciating US$ for world capital flows and foreign investment in the USA?

6 Linkages between money, output, prices and interest rates

In the UK, monetary policy has dominated the debate concerning macroeconomic policy since the mid-1970s. Increasingly, however, economists are becoming more and more sceptical about the linkages between growth in the money supply, the growth in output and inflation. The question at the forefront of the debate today concerns whether or not increases in the stock of money in circulation can lead to an increase in the economy's real output and hence reduce unemployment, or do they simply result in higher inflation?

Table 10.4 reports data on the UK's money supply, output, inflation and the rate of interest for the period 1970–92.

Questions

1. Outline the theoretical foundations for the argument that control over the growth in the money supply should reduce inflationary pressures.

Table 10.4 Money, output, inflation and interest rates.

	MO[a] (£m)	M4[a] (£m)	Output[b] (GDP, £m) current prices	Prices[c] (GDP deflator) 1990=100	Interest rates[d] (yield on Treasury bills)
1970	4,099	26,643	44,302	14.4	6.93
1971	4,289	30,976	50,034	16.0	4.46
1972	4,845	38,156	56,632	17.6	8.48
1973	5,339	46,544	65,702	19.0	12.82
1974	6,158	51,671	75,595	22.2	11.30
1975	6,873	57,943	95,587	28.3	10.93
1976	7,649	64,538	112,535	32.4	13.98
1977	8,652	74,074	129,535	36.4	6.39
1978	9,837	85,090	149,545	40.9	11.91
1979	11,014	97,339	173,194	46.1	16.49
1980	11,650	114,149	201,017	54.6	13.58
1981	11,925	137,837	218,831	60.1	15.39
1982	12,301	154,909	238,385	64.3	9.96
1983	13,038	175,462	261,225	68.0	9.04
1984	13,746	199,177	280,653	71.6	9.33
1985	14,278	225,109	307,902	75.5	11.49
1986	15,027	261,234	328,272	77.4	10.94
1987	15,664	303,006	360,675	81.3	8.38
1988	16,869	355,422	401,428	86.2	12.91
1989	17,824	422,331	441,759	92.8	15.02
1990	18,297	473,605	478,886	100.0	13.50
1991	18,850	501,791	494,824	105.8	10.45
1992	19,380	519,449	514,594	110.5	6.44

[a] End-period, amount outstanding: seasonally adjusted.
[b] Average estimates of GDP (expenditure-based) at factor cost.
[c] Implied GDP deflator based on expenditure data at factor cost.
[d] Average discount rate expressed as the rate at which interest is earned during the life of the bills.
Source: Economic Trends (London: HMSO).

2. Using the data shown in Table 10.4, graph and examine the relationship between:
   - the rate of growth of M0 and the rate of growth of prices (i.e. inflation);
   - the rate of growth of M4 and inflation.

   What difference does it make if inflation is plotted against the rate of growth of M0 and M4 lagged, say, two or three years previous and why might it make sense to do this?

3. Examine the hypothesis that monetary growth causes increases in real output in the short run.

4. How sensitive are changes in the money supply (M0 or M4) to changes in interest rates (yield on Treasury bills)?

5. Comment, in general, on the strength of monetarist economic arguments in the light of the above figures.

7 Outlook for the economy

Below is a commentary, written in mid-1995, on the state of the UK economy. It covers a broad range of macroeconomic indicators and makes reference to many of the key economic variables that have been introduced in this book. At the end of the case study there is a collection of questions that test understanding of the macroeconomy.

The current state of the economy

In the first half of 1995, the anticipated increase in interest rates has not materialized. The Chancellor's controversial decision not to raise interest rates following the May meeting with the Governor of the Bank of England seems now to have the support of the City as evidence mounts that the rate of economic growth is moderating and the Chancellor's target for an inflation rate of less than 2.5% by the spring of 1997 is achievable. This view is supported by the Treasury in its latest summer forecast published on 20 June, in which it predicts that the underlying rate of inflation (i.e. excluding mortgage interest payments) will drop to 2.5% by the end of next year. In announcing this inflation target, the Chancellor has acknowledged that at times the actual inflation rate could well rise above this target level temporarily. Indeed, this is the situation at the moment, with the publication of the retail prices index for June showing an underlying rate of 2.8%. Despite the recent slight rise, inflationary pressures remain subdued. There is good reason, therefore, for believing that the UK economy may well achieve 'a soft landing' as hoped by the government without a return to the 'boom and bust' cycle as happened so often in the past. The economic environment is steadily improving from the point of view of British business though, as we discuss below, investment in new plant and machinery is still not increasing as strongly as one might expect at this stage of the economic cycle.

The main features of the current state of the economy are as follows:

- Growth is now slowing to a more sustainable level after the unsustainable rise last year.
- Retail sales growth is modest, in the face of tough retail competition and tightening of margins in this sector generally.

- The housing market remains subdued with house prices remaining flat in some areas and falling in others, with negative equity worries being pushed to the forefront.

- The strong recovery in the manufacturing sector over the past few years is now moderating.

- Inflationary pressures are relatively subdued despite sharp increases in raw materials prices in recent months.

- Unemployment has continued to fall, standing now at around 2.3m (8.3% of the workforce), but the rate of decline is slowing down and job insecurity remains as a prominent feature of the labour market.

- Britain's unit labour costs and competitiveness have continued to improve in recent months, reflecting further improvements in productivity and moderate wage settlements. However, industrial unrest has raised its head again in recent months, notably in the rail sector. It remains to be seen whether this persists and what effect it will have on the general economic situation.

- The country's international trading performance remains strong, benefiting from sterling's competitive exchange rate in recent months.

- The latest report from the Treasury indicates a slight worsening in the PSBR position during the current financial year but the downward trend is expected to continue.

Economic forecasts for 1995 and 1996: the latest evidence
Table 10.5 sets out the economic forecasts for a number of key variables for 1995 and 1996. These forecasts are based on the latest reports made by a large number of non-governmental organizations (compiled by HM Treasury and published in June). We comment on each of the economic indicators in turn.

Economic growth
The consensus view is that economic growth has now 'come off the boil' from a peak of around 4 per cent at the end of last year. It is expected that GDP will grow by just a little over 3 per cent this year and is likely to moderate still further to just below 3 per cent in 1996. This supports the expectation of a soft landing, noted above, though it is notable that growth in the short term is still expected to remain above the UK's long-term trend rate of around 2.5 per cent.

The main driver of the above-average rate of economic growth over the past two years has been the sharp rise in export volumes relative to imports. While the UK's current account position is forecast to be more or

Table 10.5 Forecasts for the UK economy, 1995/6.[a]

Economic indicator[b]	1995	1996
Economic growth (%)	3.1	2.9
Consumers' expenditure	1.9	2.5
Fixed investment	6.1	6.2
Inflation rate (Q4; %)		
– RPI	3.7	3.4
– RPI excl MIPs[c]	3.0	3.1
Unemployment (Q4; mn)	2.19	2.01
Short-term interest rates (Q4; %)	7.44	7.66
Current account (£bn)	−0.1	−0.5
	1995/6	1996/7
PSBR (£bn financial years)	23.6	19.1

[a] Average of latest forecasts reported by 33 non-governmental organizations.
[b] Percentage changes on a year earlier unless stated otherwise.
[c] MIPs: mortgage interest payments.

less in balance over the next two years (see below), the rate of growth of exports is slowing, reflecting a general slowdown in growth for the world's developed nations. As a result, the contribution from exports to GDP growth is expected to moderate.

Consumers' expenditure

In recent months there has been a marked downward revision in forecasts for consumers' expenditure in 1995. Independent forecasts for consumers' expenditure growth in 1995, made during the first three months of the year, averaged 2.2 per cent. The average forecast now, however, made during the second quarter, is only 1.9 per cent for this year. There are a number of factors which have brought about this downward revision. The most important of these are:

- continuation of the personal sector debt overhang;
- the continued fragile state of the housing market;
- the continued effect of monetary tightness in late 1994;
- fiscal tightness;
- continued job insecurity.

There is also much media speculation about the impact that spending on the National Lottery – currently running at over £65m each week – is having on retail sales. This level of spending is equivalent to roughly 3 per cent of retail sales and has inevitably taken a proportion of spending away from the High Street shops. At the same time, however, this reduction in spending has further eased the threat of stronger retail price inflation.

Looking ahead to 1996, an upturn to 2.5 per cent growth in consumers' expenditure is expected. This reflects the anticipated impact of a number of positive factors such as:

- rising incomes as recovery continues;
- tax cuts in the November 1995 Budget;
- the impact of 'windfall gains' arising from developments such as building society mergers;
- the impact of £20 billion worth of tax-exempt special savings accounts (TESSAs) maturing in the first half of next year (equivalent to a 10p reduction in the basic rate of income tax).

The outlook for the retail sector, therefore, is likely to improve sharply during the course of the next year – this will be welcome relief for a sector which has borne the brunt of much of the recession during the early part of the 1990s.

Investment
The outlook for investment in fixed assets is expected to continue to improve slightly over the next eighteen months. The average forecasts for 1995 and 1996 stand at a little over 6 per cent growth despite cutbacks in housing starts and public sector investment. This rise in investment is likely to be concentrated in the corporate sector, prompted by strong profit growth, large corporate financial surpluses and increased capacity utilization. In particular, manufacturing investment is strengthening as capacity constraints are now becoming evident. Investment growth by financial sector organizations is especially strong. However, it should be noted that the rate of capital investment growth in general is taking place from a low post-recession base and is regarded by many observers as insufficient to sustain general economic growth above its longer-term trend without the emergence of stronger inflationary pressures over the medium term. A fine balance has to be maintained between the sustainability of economic growth and continued downward pressure on inflation.

Inflation
Table 10.5 shows forecasts for the headline rate of retail price inflation (RPI) as well as the 'underlying' rate (i.e. RPI excluding mortgage interest payments). It is the latter which is the basis for the government's target rate

of inflation. The Chancellor's target has two components – a range for underlying inflation of 1–4 per cent and a subsidiary commitment to get inflation below 2.5 per cent by the spring of 1997. It will be seen that underlying inflation is expected to remain at around 3 per cent during the course of this year and next year. If inflationary pressures remain subdued, as forecast, there will be no need for further tightening of monetary policy. On balance, the Chancellor's gamble in not raising interest rates in recent months would seem to have paid off – at least in the short term. It will be recalled that there was much media attention surrounding the (unannounced) disagreement between the Chancellor and the Governor of the Bank of England in May (and to a lesser extent in June). Fortunately, this did not develop into the financial crisis feared at the time.

Unemployment

The latest monthly figures for unemployment indicate that the rate of decline has continued to moderate: the total fell by 49,000 in the three months to May compared with a fall of 145,000 in Q4 1994. The official unemployment rate now stands at around 8.3 per cent of the workforce and is now more than 650,000 below its December 1992 peak. This trend is in line with the softening of overall economic growth. However, there remains a consensus among forecasters that the unemployment total will continue to decline over the next eighteen months, albeit at a diminishing pace, with the level falling to around two million by the fourth quarter of 1996. However, it must be borne in mind that much of this improvement is in large measure due to an increase in part-time employment and a decline in the number of people registering for unemployment benefits. The latter point is significant since the decline in the registered unemployed total has not been matched by an increase in the number of new jobs created. The downward pressure on the numbers unemployed is likely to be maintained by the continued tightening of the benefits system. This will also dampen wage pressures which will further help to keep down the rate of inflation.

Falls in the jobless total during the past two years have been greatest in the southern half of the country (excluding Greater London): for example, between 1993 and 1995 the unemployment total fell by around 28 per cent in the South-east region, 26 per cent in the South-west, 21 per cent in East Anglia and 26 per cent in the West Midlands. It is expected that the largest falls will continue in the South-east outside of London and the South-west as well as in Scotland over the course of the next few years.

Interest rates

While interest rates have not been raised in recent months, market speculation remains that a further tightening in monetary conditions is inevitable if inflationary pressures are to be adequately restrained. Any further rise, however, will be marginal and, in general, the consensus forecast is that short-term interest rates will peak during the course of the next eighteen months at a little over 7.5 per cent. Indeed, it could well turn out to be the case that this forecast will be at the top end of the range since US interest rates have begun to edge downwards following a cut of 0.25 per cent by the Federal Reserve Bank on 7 July. This was the consequence of reports showing that the pace of economic growth in the USA is beginning to moderate.

Naturally, this scenario for UK interest rates will be welcome news for UK plc as well as for the personal sector. It is unlikely, however, that this will be sufficient to provide a major stimulus to particular sectors such as the housing market in the short term – a much more fundamental boost to confidence is required in this respect such as a major initiative from the government to kick-start activity.

Current account

One of the remarkable features of the UK's economic recovery has been the improvement in the current account of the balance of payments. Despite a forecast slowdown in the growth of exports, the independent forecasters, on average, are expecting the current account to more or less remain in balance over the next two years. A major feature of this performance is the significant contribution made by both the oil and non-oil trade sectors. Looking further ahead to beyond 1996, we can expect the current account to show a growing deficit as consumer spending continues to recover, but this is not thought likely to pose a serious threat to the economy.

All too often in the past a current account deficit has forced the government at this stage in the recovery cycle to tighten monetary policy in order to reduce consumers' demand for imports. Independent forecasters now seem agreed that the current account will not be a constraint on continued economic growth and this is a further factor leading to only modest upward pressure on interest rates.

The government's borrowing position

The consensus view among independent forecasters is that the government's borrowing position will turn out at around £23bn over the financial year ending April 1996, falling to just over £19bn by April 1997. The Treasury's original forecast made in the last Budget was for a PSBR of £21.5bn during the current financial year, but this has now been revised up to £23.5bn, as reported in the Treasury's Summer Economic Forecast – based on the assumption that there are no tax cuts. This revision reflects the fact that there has been a shortfall in government tax receipts and an increase in government expenditure as the pace of economic growth has begun to moderate.

Most observers anticipate tax cuts in the next Budget and this will make it more difficult for the government to secure a larger reduction in the PSBR in the run-up to the next election. Much depends on the extent to which the government can control its expenditure in the next two years. On balance, it seems that the financial markets' fears about the government's budget deficit may increase marginally. Given the government's political dilemma, however, it is unlikely that the PSBR will be a major constraint on the Chancellor's ability to reduce taxes next year. But he will have to make a fine judgement concerning the precise scope for such reductions. While modest tax cuts will help to secure the continuation of the recovery in demand throughout 1996 and may help to boost the government's political popularity, large tax cuts may raise the financial markets' fears of inflation and force a further tightening in monetary policy.

The feel-good factor remains elusive

The general outlook for the economy is one of continued recovery centred on exports and a gradual improvement in investment, with a strengthening contribution from consumers' expenditure taking over as the main engine of growth in 1996. The main conclusion we draw from the economic situation outlined above is that, while we may see interest rates edge up again in the coming months, fears of substantially higher rates have now generally subsided. Despite a slight rise in inflation over recent months, we believe that competitive pressures in retail markets, together with continued impressive growth of labour productivity and flexibility, will ensure that inflation remains close to the government's target range in the medium term.

All the recovery now lacks is the notoriously elusive 'feel-good' factor. This lack of confidence on the part of consumers is largely attributable to the continuing lack of a visible recovery in the housing market. Concern has deepened in the housebuilding sector following an optimistic outlook at the beginning of last year. The gloom in the housing sector has increased following the announcement by a major builder (Lovells) that it is to pull out of private sector housebuilding altogether and focus on building for local authorities and housing associations. On balance, it is likely that the return of a 'feel-good' factor will remain elusive for the rest of this year but we can expect to see an improvement coming through in 1996.

Questions

1. What do you think is meant by 'a soft landing' in the context of economic activity?

2. What evidence can you find in the report to support the prediction of a 'soft landing'?

3. The UK experienced a severe 'boom and bust' cycle in the late 1980s and early 1990s. What were the main causes of such volatile activity? What were the main consequences for the economy and for economic policy?

4. Monetary policy has tended to emphasize small changes in short-term interest rates in recent years. Explain the rationale behind this policy and compare it with interest-rate policy decisions in the 1980s.

5. How has the UK managed to achieve such a dramatic improvement in its export competitiveness during the first half of the 1990s? What are the longer-term prospects for the current account of the balance of payments?

6. Why is the continued fragile state of the housing market regarded as an important factor with respect to consumers' expenditure and the general 'feel-good' factor?

7. Why should the financial markets be concerned about the government's budget deficit position?

8. How have supply-side policies changed the UK's economic performance in recent years?

Appendix: Sources of economic data for managers

This appendix gives details of the principal sources of UK economic data as well as the key international sources of data. The UK data are categorized according to the following headings:

1. general;
2. economic growth;
3. personal income and saving;
4. industry and commerce;
5. labour statistics;
6. inflation;
7. housing and construction;
8. money, banking and finance;
9. the balance of payments.

Two useful guides to UK statistical sources are available:

1. *Government Statistics: A Brief Guide to Sources* (London: Information Services Division, Cabinet Office) (free)
2. CSO, *Guide to Official Statistics* (London: HMSO, occasional).

UK sources

1. General
Annual Abstract of Statistics, HMSO.
Bank of England Quarterly Bulletin, Bank of England.
Economic Trends, HMSO. Monthly and annual supplement.

Financial Statistics, HMSO. Monthly.
Monthly Digest of Statistics, HMSO.
UK National Accounts, HMSO. Annually.
Regional Trends, HMSO. Annually.
Social Trends, HMSO. Annually.

2. Economic growth
Economic Trends, tables 6, 8, 26, 28, 68–71. Special section January, April, July and October.
Monthly Digest of Statistics, tables 1.1–1.3, 7.1.
UK National Accounts, sections 1–3.

3. Personal income and saving
Economic Trends, tables 10, 12, 14.
Financial Statistics, section 9.
Monthly Digest of Statistics, tables 1.5, 14.1, 14.2.
UK National Accounts, section 4.

4. Industry and commerce
Business Monitor MA3, Business Statistics Office. Annually.
Economic Trends, tables 16, 18, 22, 60, 62.
Financial Statistics, section 8.
Monthly Digest of Statistics, tables 1.7–1.9.
Reports on the Census of Production – Business Monitor PA Series, HMSO. Annually.
UK National Accounts, section 5.

5. Labour statistics
Economic Trends, tables 34, 36, 38, 40.
Employment Gazette, HMSO. Monthly.
Labour Force Survey Quarterly Bulletin, HMSO. Quarterly.
New Earnings Survey, HMSO. Annually.
Monthly Digest of Statistics, section 3.

6. Inflation
Economic Trends, tables 5, 42.
Employment Gazette, tables 6.1–6.7.
Family Expenditure Survey, Department of Employment, HMSO. Annually.
Inflation Report, Bank of England. Quarterly.

Monthly Digest of Statistics, tables 18.1–18.6.
Price Index Numbers for Current Cost Accounting, HMSO (annually) and
Business Monitor MM17, HMSO (monthly) for wholesale price indices.

7. Housing and construction
Housing and Construction Statistics, HMSO. Annually and quarterly.

8. Money, banking and finance
Abstract of Banking Statistics, City of London and Scottish Banks (CLSB).
Annually.
Bank of England Quarterly Bulletin, statistical annex.
Economic Trends, tables 52, 54, 56, 64, 66.
Financial Statistics, sections 3, 6, 7, 11.
BSA Bulletin, Building Societies Association; now *Housing Finance,* Council
of Mortgage Lenders. Quarterly.

9. The balance of payments
Bank of England Quarterly Bulletin, statistical annex, sections 14–18, 'External
balance sheet of the UK', annual article, September or August issue.
British Council for Invisible Exports, *Annual Report.*
Economic Trends, tables 46, 48, 50, and quarterly balance of payments article
in March, June, September and December issues.
Financial Statistics, section 10 and tables 13.1–13.3.
Monthly Review of External Trade Statistics, and *Annual Supplement,* DTI.
The Overseas Trade Statistics of the United Kingdom, HMSO. Monthly and
annually.
Overseas Trade Analysed in Terms of Industries, Business Monitor MQ10,
HMSO Quarterly.
The United Kingdom Balance of Payments (Pink Book), HMSO. Annually.

International sources

There is a very large number of sources of international data. A
comprehensive guide, arranged according to subject, is:

*Instat–International Statistics Sources: A Subject Guide to Sources of International
Comparative Statistics* by M.C. Fleming and J.G. Nellis, London: Routledge,
1995.

General

UN Statistical Year Book and *UN National Accounts Statistics*, United Nations (UN), New York. Annually.

Yearbook of Labour Statistics, International Labour Organization (ILO), Geneva. Annually.

International Financial Statistics, International Monetary Fund (IMF), Washington. Monthly.

National Accounts, Organization for Economic Co-operation and Development (OECD), Paris. Annually.

European Community

A wide range of statistics publications is published by the Statistical Office of the European Communities (SOEC) in Luxembourg. Selected titles are given below:

Basic Statistics of the Community. Annually.
Industry: Statistical yearbook.
Industrial Trends: Monthly statistics.
Industrial Production: Quarterly statistics.
Structure and Activity of Industry. Annually.
Earnings: Industry and services. Half-yearly.
Labour Force Survey. Annually.
National Accounts, 3 volumes. Annually.
External Trade: Statistical yearbook. Annually.

A full listing of EC statistical sources is available in *Eurostat Catalogue*, free from Eurostat and from the Office of Official Publications of the European Communities, Luxembourg.

Further reading

The following recommended books are divided into two groups: (1) those which are aimed at the economics non-specialist and which are, therefore, of a more general, non-technical, nature and (2) those which are more specialist texts intended for serious students of economics and which require some previous grounding in economic theory. There are many books available which fall into both categories but we have been selective in identifying those which we feel are the most readable.

(a) General texts
Chrystal, K.A., *Controversies in Macroeconomics*, 2nd edn (Oxford: Philip Allan, 1983).

Donaldson, P. and Farquhar, J., *Understanding the British Economy* (Harmondsworth: Penguin, 1988).

Johnson, C., *Measuring the Economy* (London: Macmillan, 1988).

Kay, J.A. and King, M.A., *The British Tax System*, 5th edn (Oxford: Oxford University Press, 1990).

Keegan, W., *Mrs Thatcher's Economic Experiment* (Harmondsworth: Penguin, 1984).

Pratten, C., *Applied Macroeconomics* (Oxford: Oxford University Press, 1985).

Robinson, P., *The Unbalanced Recovery* (Oxford: Philip Allan, 1988).

Shaw, G.K., *Keynesian Economics: The permanent revolution* (Aldershot: Edward Elgar, 1988).

(b) Specialist texts
Begg, D., Fischer, S. and Dornbusch, R., *Economics*, 4th edn (London: McGraw-Hill, 1994).

Curwen, P. (ed), *Understanding the UK Economy*, 3rd edn (Hampshire: Macmillan, 1994).

Hardwick, P., Khan, B. and Longmead, J., *An Introduction to Modern Economics*, 4th edn (London: Longman, 1994).

Parkin, M. and King, D., *Economics* (Wokingham: Addison-Wesley, 1992).

Powell, R., *Economics for Professional and Business Studies*, 2nd edn (London, DP Publications Ltd, 1993).

Sloman, J., *Economics* (Cambridge: Harvester Wheatsheaf, 1991).

Index